M000098367

The Enneagram for Managers

The Enneagram for Managers

Nine different perspectives on managing people

Oscar David

Writers Club Press

San Jose New York Lincoln Shanghai

The Enneagram for Managers
Nine Different Perspectives on Managing People

All Rights Reserved. Copyright © 2001 Oscar David Consultancy B.V.,
Amsterdam, The Netherlands

No part of this book may be reproduced or transmitted in any form or by
any means, graphic, electronic, or mechanical, including photocopying,
recording, taping, or by any information storage retrieval system, without
the permission in writing from the publisher.

⸍ Translation: Christine Hayes

Writers Club Press
an imprint of iUniverse.com, Inc.

For information address:
iUniverse.com, Inc.
5220 S 16th, Ste. 200
Lincoln, NE 68512
www.iuniverse.com

ISBN: 0-595-19546-6

Printed in the United States of America

CONTENTS

S

PREFACE

I believe that success greatly depends on the ability to understand the motivation behind our own behavior and that of others. This book presents a method of developing this ability. It has proved helpful to me and also to the many managers and professional people with whom I have worked as a management consultant. My view is that in gaining better insight into human behavior, the achievement of success and satisfaction in our work and in life in general can acquire greater meaning.

It was in 1992 that I first heard about the method known as the Enneagram. A colleague returned from California, bringing with her a remarkable book that she wanted me to read: The Enneagram: Understanding Yourself and the Others in Your Life. The book defined nine different personality types, the premise being that we all have the nine types in us, but that one of the nine is more applicable to each individual than the others. Of course, as a psychologist, I'm familiar with personality typologies, so I wasn't particularly impatient to discover another variation on the theme.

But although I had some reservations at the beginning, it wasn't long before I was thoroughly enthralled. The types were described according to their behavior, and also in terms of the motivation for that behavior. It was clear how different types might demonstrate identical behavior for entirely different reasons. I was impressed how recognizable the examples of the nine types were, and how this gave me more insight into others and myself. Thoroughly fascinated, I wanted to learn more. I contacted the author of the book, Helen Palmer, and went to California several times to study with Helen and her colleague David

Daniels, learning to become an Enneagram trainer. My interest in the Enneagram grew rapidly, far beyond being a favorite topic of conversation at parties. My clients also became interested in the subject, wanting to know more about my new insights.

Before long, the Enneagram was integrated into team-building sessions, management development programs and executive coaching. I saw how many of the participants made the same discovery as I had: that the Enneagram is an inspiring framework, that continually gives fresh insight into how we 'work'. This book is based on my workshop experience with managers and professionals in a large number of international organizations. Some of the examples and quotes have been altered to preserve their anonymity.

The book can be used in a number of different ways. You may find it a useful introduction to the Enneagram. You could also use it as a short 'workshop' of your own. You will be able to explore your own Enneagram-type, and you may find it interesting to study the answers to some of the questions asked by your colleagues in management. The book is above all intended to encourage and help you in the further development of your self-knowledge and understanding of others.

For the sake of simplicity, I have used the pronoun 'he' in most cases, where either 'he' or 'she' could apply.

ACKNOWLEDGEMENTS

Firstly, I would like to thank Chohan Neale, through whom I first heard about the Enneagram. My thanks go to all pioneers of the Enneagram, particularly Helen Palmer and A.H. Almaas. My thanks too, to all of my clients and participants in my workshops, for the opportunity they offered me to gain the experience on which this book is based.

My thanks to Jennifer Cronick, Hans Jeths, Evert Jan Karman, Katja Staartjes, Connie Veul and Theo Ybema for their stimulating support in discussions of earlier versions of this book. Additional thanks to Mina Janssen, for her patience in working through each revision and as always, helping everything to come together in the end.

I would also like to thank Rob Heiligers, Klazinus Lagerwerf, Marjan van Lier, Frank Post and Robert Rubinstein for their useful ideas and helpful suggestions about the approach and contents of the book.

Also my thanks to Christine Hayes, Manya McClew, Peter Koenig, Robert Rogers and Coen van der Kroon for their support and efforts to make this version available in English.

My special thanks go to Daan van Kampenhout. His boundless trust and inspirational encouragement have been of enormous support during the writing of this book.

I wish you great pleasure in reading it.

Oscar David

INTRODUCTION

Why do some managers always seem to have the boss's ear, while others don't seem to be able to get anywhere with him? How come some team leaders always find support for the unpopular changes they introduce, but others are more likely to be faced with resistance? What is the reason why some managers can effortlessly acquire and maintain a good customer network, while others have to struggle every inch of the way?

In many of these situations, it is not professional expertise alone that allows the successful to achieve the results they want, but also insight into their own behavior and that of others. In my view, the achievement of a high degree of insight into behavior and motivation is potentially possible for everyone. I would like to demonstrate with this book how your increased awareness of this potential could help you in your work.

A bit of psychology

No two people are alike. You don't have to be a psychologist to come to this conclusion. I have certainly never met an exact twin of myself, and presumably neither have you. People may resemble each other in some way, but in reality they are quite different from each other. The question is, how does this happen? Why are we so different from each other? How, in fact, do we come to be who we are?

There are different theories about this:

1. Who we are is a result of our upbringing, the 'nurture' theory. By nurture, what is meant here is our upbringing in the widest sense of the word, involving not only the influence of our parents, but also that of

teachers, society at large, our national or regional culture and the beliefs with which we grow up.

2. Personality is largely inherited: the 'nature' theory. You will often hear belief in this view expressed in the comment: 'He has been like that ever since he was a baby.'

3. Personality is a combination of nature and nurture.

4. Personality is a result of what happened in previous lives: karma and reincarnation. This may sound a bit exotic, but it is a view taken by many of the world's population.

5. Our personality is determined by a combination of all of the above.

The viewpoint on which this book is based is that people have an inherent tendency towards certain qualities and weaknesses. Taken as a whole, these qualities and drawbacks constitute the personality. This line of thought means that it is irrelevant which of the above theories you favor. The question now is how predisposition towards a specific personality type leads to the development of specific qualities and weaknesses.

As an analogy, imagine a human baby in the first months of life as a circle. Now, I am not a father myself, but I am regularly invited to make the acquaintance of new arrivals in the families of my friends and relatives. Contemplation of the new life usually moves me deeply. I sometimes wonder if I'm the only one to experience these sentiments, although I suspect that most of those present succumb to the same experience. It is interesting to hear how those most closely involved express their feelings. The new-born baby is frequently described as 'pure beauty', 'pure love' or 'pure trust'. A new-born child seems to embody qualities that we perceive to be pure, or uncontaminated.

Now let's see what happens later on in at the child's life. As an example, one of my clients—I'll call him Ben—told me that he grew up in the country. When I asked Ben what he could remember of the first years of life, he could not recall many memories. However, there was one in particular that he remembered in vivid detail. When he was only about one or two years old, an important event occurred in the daily life of the small community where he lived. The days of pre-planned, boring trips to the next biggest town, some 40 miles away, came to an end. A shopping center was opened on the very outskirts of the village, bringing impulse buying and last minute shopping within easy reach of its inhabitants. On the day of the grand opening, Ben's mother wheeled him the short distance to the new shops in his baby-buggy, thrilled to have variety and convenience on her doorstep at last. Of course, everyone else from the village was there. Ben's mother enjoyed some window-shopping and went to the supermarket for her groceries; chatted with some neighbors she met there and returned home, very pleased with the new development. Once home, however, she was overcome with the uneasy feeling of having forgotten something important. To her shock, she suddenly realized that she had forgotten all about little Ben. Horrified, she ran back to the supermarket, only to discover that the shop had already closed.

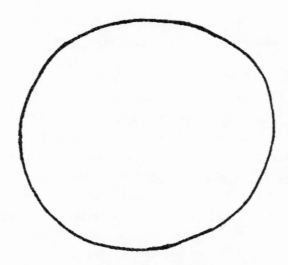

Fig. 1: Perfect Circle

From a psychological point of view, being left behind in the super-market is a far-reaching affair. To all intents and purposes, Ben is now no longer protected by his mother. He is thrown on the mercy of the outside world. Up to this point still a perfect circle *(Fig. 1)*, Ben now experiences trauma *(Fig. 2)*. In medical science, trauma is a physical wound. Although Ben, in this example, is not physically wounded, what he experiences is a psychological wound. It is all very well to be pure love, trust and hope, but that doesn't protect you from being wounded. Ben therefore has to develop a successful survival strategy. Metaphorically speaking, he builds a construction over the wound to stop the bleeding. This construction eventually grows into a fortress, and this is Ben's personality *(Fig. 3)*.

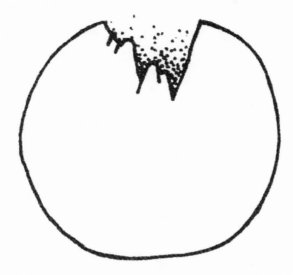

Fig. 2: Trauma

The personality contains a strategy intended to help us achieve success in life and at work, and to avoid unpleasant experiences. The good news is that it helps us to deal with our surroundings sensibly. If we had no personality and remained pure love, hope and trust, our chances of survival would probably be slight. The bad news is that the personality has only a limited repertoire. No matter how convinced we may be that our way of thinking, feeling and acting is unique, in practice you will notice how predictable people's reactions are, when we are familiar with their character.

In a sense, the personality is comparable to the masks used in Greek tragedy. The word personal is in fact derived from the Greek word for mask, *persona*. The Ancient Greeks used masks to allow actors to fulfill their roles more easily in the dramas they enacted. The masks made it more difficult for the public to see the true identity of the actor, but that was precisely the point: all attention was diverted to the role the actor was playing. The personality works more or less the same way, psychologically speaking.

Fig. 3: Fortress

The following pages describe a method of identifying the different kinds of masks people wear. You can see which mask fits you best. It might be interesting to explore how to make better use of it.

The Enneagram

The Enneagram is an efficacious model that describes nine different views on life. Ennea is the Greek word for nine, and a grammos is a model.

You will recognize some of your own attitudes in all of the perspectives, depending on the situation you are in. Experience proves, however, that the more a person studies the different perspectives, the more obvious it becomes that some of them are more personally applicable than others. In fact, most of us discover one particular strategy that seems to match our own closely. This doesn't mean that we don't recognize and even employ other perspectives on occasion; it is just that they don't come so naturally to us, or we only use them in certain circumstances. The following brief exercise will demonstrate my point.

Exercise

Put the book down for a moment, so as to leave your hands free. Now cross your arms. Presumably you will find this easy to do. Now cross your arms the other way around. You may have to think about this first, but you won't find it difficult to do either.

When I asked you to cross your arms the first time, you didn't need to think about it: the action was automatic. You didn't say to yourself: "Now I'm going to cross my arms. That's interesting. There are different ways to do that. Which one shall I choose today?" You just crossed your arms. You were operating on automatic pilot, so to speak. The second attempt probably took a little more effort. Not, that you weren't able to carry out the action, but you quite likely thought about it briefly first.

The same is true for our natural Enneagram perspective; we assume our preferred viewpoint automatically. There is no effort involved, and we are hardly even aware of it. Just as we are normally not really aware of how we usually cross our arms. As soon as we become aware of our choice of perspective, however, we can make better use of the qualities, which, according to the Enneagram, are inherent to it. We are also better able to anticipate the pitfalls that this perspective entails. Furthermore, it is easier to let go of our usual perspective once we see that we have a choice.

The Enneagram perspective is derived from the personality, which develops in the first years of our lives. As already mentioned, my view is that people are predisposed towards a specific perspective. Certain experiences, being left behind on a shopping spree, for instance, reinforce the development of a specific pattern according to an individual's predisposition towards a specific mode of reaction. Identical experiences can therefore trigger different modes of reaction, due to differences in predisposition.

Exercise

Which attributes would those who know you best, both privately and at work, use to describe you? Make a list of these qualities.

Then make a list of weaker points they might mention.

Now select five positive qualities and five weaknesses that you agree with. Keep this description at hand while reading the next chapter, to help you identify your own type.

Models as maps

This book presents a model that describes human behavior and the motivation behind it. Bear in mind that it is a model, not the reality. At best, a model can only describe situations so that we are better able to recognize reality, and benefit from the description. The Enneagram is like a map, intended to help us understand human motivation better. Don't be tempted into confusing the map with the territory. It is merely a tool to guide us in the right direction.

How this book is organized

The book is a guide to the Enneagram and its potential for use.

Part 1 presents a bird's-eye view of the different types, so that you can make acquaintance with the Enneagram and learn more about yourself and others from a different point of view. You can use this part of the book to help identify your own type. The descriptions function as a checklist against your own experience, and you may recognize them as being applicable now or at some other period in your life. You may also enjoy reflecting on which people you know who might fit the descriptions.

Part 2 gives the answers to a selection of questions that have been put to me in recent years during workshops and consultancy discussions. These questions deal with the Enneagram as a model, the Enneagram in companies and organizations and methods of working with the Enneagram. This section offers you the possibility of furthering your knowledge through the experiences of other managers and professionals. It is also intended to provide more insight into the relationship between the Enneagram and personal development.

Part 3 is an extensive bibliography. I have included a short review of the books mentioned in order to help you choose appropriate books for your continued exploration of the Enneagram.

PART 1

NINE DIFFERENT PERSPECTIVES ON MANAGING PEOPLE

This part of the book introduces each type in different ways. Each chapter is organized so as to give you a quick overview of the type in the sub-sections 'Type number and name', 'The supermarket', 'What others appreciate in this type', 'What others find problematic about this type', 'Nationality type', and 'Self-assessment'. The additional sections go into more detail, to help you to become more familiar with each type.

Type number and name

The types are numbered from 1 to 9. Each number also has a name. One of the interesting aspects of the Enneagram is that it is not a nor-mative model, meaning that no type is considered better than any other is. Any type can be a good manager. The differences between them refer to the extent to which a person has developed the qualities related to a specific type, or become stuck in its pitfalls. The names given to each type will probably give rise to associations; some names may sound more positive or negative than others. Because this is definitely not the intention, it is usually the type number that is referred to throughout the description, rather than the name given to it.

The Supermarket

Under each type you will find an indication of what Ben's response to the supermarket incident might be, if he were that type.

What others appreciate

This is a list of five qualities or other aspects that others appreciate about a type. It is of course not complete, and only the most frequently named aspects are listed. By 'others' is meant colleagues, associates, managers or bosses and clients.

What others find problematic

Here too, the most frequently mentioned aspects are listed. Some people may discover more qualities and others more flaws in themselves or others. Again, 'others' refers to colleagues, associates, managers and customers.

Nationality type

Every country has its own characteristics, and therefore could be said to represent an Enneagram-type. Naturally, this by no means indicates that most people from that country belong to that specific Enneagram-type. However, a number of aspects of the culture can help to clarify what the nationality type is. One or two countries where the characteristics of the type play an important role in that culture are indicated for each type. Organizations often embody the characteristics of the nationality type of their country of origin.

Self-assessment

The self-assessment shows one way in which a type might describe himself. The description given here is a compilation of the most frequently mentioned aspects given by people of this type. You may find that some of the qualities mentioned have not blossomed in yourself in quite the same way, or that failings are described that you mastered long ago. Don't let this throw you off the scent.

Issues

This is a discussion of the six most frequently occurring issues for each type. Each theme is related to particular qualities and failings. One issue may highlight the qualities, while another may focus more frequently on the failings. Your personal experience could well contain a difference balance of the two than in the examples chosen. You may recognize some issues from the past, or conversely, they may have only recently come to light. Since this book focuses primarily on how to achieve greater understanding in the workplace, only a few examples of private and personal situations have been selected. Naturally, they could equally well apply to the private sphere. The quotes and examples cited for each issue are from real people: other managers and professionals. In some cases, a few details have been altered, only to preserve the anonymity of their source.

Management style

Attitudes towards management have been given for each type. This does not mean that this type always acts in that way. In spite of the fact that a specific type may be more inclined towards relationship-oriented coaching, it could well be that he has learned to be task-oriented in certain situations.

Under pressure or stress

This is a description of how each type might think, feel and act under pressure or stress. The theory of the Enneagram is that the characteristics of another type are assumed in times of stress or when under pressure. Following the direction of the arrow on the line between the types, as illustrated on the Enneagram model, reveals which type this is.

Relaxed or safe

When relaxed or secure, the type follows a different line, against the direction of the arrow. This sub-section discusses which elements of another type are assumed in these situations.

Organizational characteristics

Companies and institutions also frequently have specific characteristics that play an important part in the organizational culture. Eight characteristics are listed for each type.

How to deal with a particular type

This section offers five suggestions for improved co-operation with a manager, associate, colleague or client of the type discussed. Almost all the suggestions were offered by managers and professionals of the relevant type during workshops, when asked what tips they would suggest to improve communication with their type. That does not mean that the suggestions will be applicable for everyone of this type; there is no infallible recipe for this. Always check first with the person in question. If possible, ask whether he thinks that the suggestion would work for him. In fact, you might like to ask whether they have any suggestions of their own. Apart from contributing to the dialogue, there's always the possibility that they are not the type you thought they were!

Suggestions for development

Each chapter includes a list of four suggestions for further development of each type. These are interesting possibilities for the types themselves, and could also be used by a manager or coach to encourage the development of staff of this type. Here too, the suggestions are those offered by other managers and professionals during the course of workshops, as ways in which to optimize their own effectiveness. They are not intended as a substitute for careful assessment on your part. Check first whether the suggestion is applicable for you. You may have better ideas. And if you should decide to offer the suggestion to an associate, even greater care is advisable. It might be wise to check first what he thinks of it.

TYPE 1

The Improver

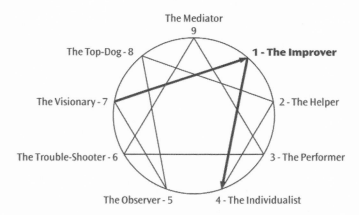

The Mediator
9
The Top-Dog - 8
1 - The Improver
The Visionary - 7
2 - The Helper
The Trouble-Shooter - 6
3 - The Performer
The Observer - 5
4 - The Individualist

Left behind in the supermarket, Type 1 thinks to himself

"This could have been handled better. If there were a decent infant-detector system at the entrance to the supermarket, the problem wouldn't occur. It's easy. The system registers each mother and infant entering the supermarket. If either the mother or the infant leaves alone, an alarm goes

off. Maybe I should do the work myself, to make sure that all baby-buggies are properly equipped...."

What others appreciate in Type 1

- A good eye for detail
- Keeps to agreements
- Sense of responsibility
- Never loses sight of principles
- Knows just how things ought to be

What others find difficult in Type 1

- Can be very principled and tenacious
- Has difficulty delegating
- Good is seldom good enough
- Always knows better
- Doesn't always find it easy to relax

Type 1 National culture

- Switzerland
- Singapore

Type 1 Self-description

"Ever since I was young, I've always known the right way to do things. It's like that in my work, too. When I see a letter written by my associate, I immediately spot the mistakes. The tone of voice is wrong. And it's full of grammatical errors. You wouldn't believe how many highly trained people can't write a decent letter. I know it would be best to give the letter back with suggestions for improvement, and let them handle it, come what may. But since it's in my hands now, I might as well just do it myself. I'm working on it anyway, and it absolutely has to go out in today's mail. It isn't good enough to let something this important get delayed. There was a time

when I would have been disappointed in my associate, but now I talk these matters over carefully during appraisals. There are more important things to worry about. There's so much here than needs improvement, there's no end to it. It's crazy really, how easy-going some of my colleagues are, when the organization is under such pressure. I quite enjoy the appreciation that is shown for my efforts. They may think I'm very critical and fussy, but they know I'm good at what I do. I know I have a few failings that could do with correction, but compared to others, I do very well. I think I'm appreciated in this company for my sense of responsibility. The quality of my work is uncontested."

Issues for Type 1

• Sense of responsibility

Type 1 often has a greater sense of responsibility than the average employee. Which although all very well, can lead to excessive overwork. For Type 1, a job is seldom done well enough or ever really complete.

"I worked until 3 am again yesterday, writing up a proposal for a client. Even though I knew we would get the order anyway. I know I should take things more easily, but, well, once I've started something, my honor is at stake if it's not perfect."

• Delegation

It is difficult to delegate without confidence in the other person to do the job properly.

"As director of the company, I know I should be able to delegate more. I could easily have one of my associates write up my speeches, for example. But I don't do that very often. I suspect I'd spend more time correcting it than if I just write it myself."

• Meeting expectations

Type 1 often doesn't only demand a lot of himself, he is also demanding of his co-workers. Colleagues may often have the feeling that what they do is never good enough, because they never seem to meet his expectations. This impression is reinforced through Type 1's habitual focus on improvement. He is quick to point out where things are going wrong and what could be better. It can be useful to have a Type 1 manager point out areas for improvement, but it doesn't always make people feel very motivated. Type 1 managers need to remember to give credit where it is due.

"When I have an appraisal or find out through 360° feedback sessions how my staff see me, the picture is an interesting one. Outstanding people like it that I give them a sense of direction. Average staff members have more difficulties with me—and of course, the majority falls into this category. They find me overly critical and say that I don't encourage them. I worry about this sometimes, because naturally, that is not my intention."

Not only staff members, but bosses and co-managers of Type 1 seldom come up to his standards. Type 1 needs to recognize his disappointment in the mediocre level of his own boss, directors, co-managers or the organization as a whole, if he is not to find himself continually in conflict about it. Many examples of Type 1 managers leave their jobs because of the 'below standard' achievements of others. But changing jobs doesn't always solve the problem.

"Everyone is wildly enthusiastic about me in this company, but I've had enough of it. I seem to be the only one who makes any effort to clear up all the mess that my predecessors left behind them."

• Indignation

Type 1 can become very indignant and angry if things don't go the way they think they should. They are not always aware of this themselves, which can create an unnecessary distance, particularly with their staff.

"My staff sometimes find me very strict, almost like a schoolmaster. Especially when things are not going the way I think they should, according to them. Personally, I thought I wasn't too bad about that."

• Forming judgments and knowing better

Type 1 sees what is right and what is not. Consequently, he makes fast judgments. His colleagues, staff and managers may get the impression that he does not welcome discussion, so Type 1 just goes ahead and explains exactly how things are. Others may not particularly want to hear this and come to the conclusion that Type 1 always thinks he knows better. They may easily overlook the fact that Type 1 is laboring under the impression that he ought to know better. He doesn't only target his external environment with his know-it-all voice.

"My parents once told me an anecdote about when I was five years old. It was my birthday party. All my friends were allowed to choose what color beaker they wanted for their lemonade. The little girl from next door pointed to one of them and said, "I want the red one." I immediately corrected her, telling her "That's not red, it's pink." I was right, but my parents were a little concerned as to the wisdom of this type of comment. I'm still like that. I'm quick to see what is right and what is wrong, and sometimes I have to hold myself back so as not to correct others. I've learned that there is a difference between being right and setting others straight."

• Relaxation

It is not always easy for a Type 1 to relax. Work is more important than pleasure. An extra week's holiday often helps more than a few afternoons off. After all, what do you need an afternoon off for, where there is still work to be done...?

"I relax when I'm on holiday. And weekend trips are wonderful. When I come home from work in the evening there is usually a lot going on there, and the weekends are pretty full as well."

Management style

Type 1 generally has clearly-defined ideas and standards about what constitutes a good manager. The ideas may vary, but you usually know what you can expect from them.

"My management style is straightforward and I like to be involved. I expect things to run well and that my staff will call on me when they need me. Meanwhile, I always know what's going on. I have to restrain myself from interfering too much sometimes. Especially with somewhat less competent employees."

Under pressure or stress: Shift to 4

Type 1 moves in the direction of Type 4 when under pressure or feeling stress. The characteristics of Type 4 that may then appear are:
• Surfacing emotions, like anger or sadness;
• Feeling misunderstood and alone.

"I usually give a cheerful impression. I'm well organized and work hard. I don't show that it's getting too much for me until I really cannot take it any longer. Then I get angry, sad and almost unpredictable. People around me hardly recognize me. Luckily, that hardly ever happens at work."

Relaxed: Shift to 7

Type 1 moves in the direction of 7 when in a relaxed state. The characteristics of Type 7 that may then appear are:
- Enjoyment of the moment;
- Less bound by rules, standards and sense of responsibility.

"I'm quite different when I'm on holiday. I take at least three weeks. Once I'm away, I could stay there forever. My family finds me much nicer then, I'm more unconstrained and more humorous, I enjoy myself."

Type 1 Organizational characteristics

- Superior quality
- High standards
- Quality improvement is central
- Products not cheap, but the best
- Hard work, lots of overtime, few distractions
- Superiority: We know what's good for our customers
- Focus on principles
- Good internal organization

How to get along with Type 1

- Don't take Type 1's critical attitude too personally; he's probably just as critical of himself.
- Ask what his values and standards are, so that you can take them into account.
- It's not usually obvious when things are too much for Type 1. Managers need to be on the lookout for this and discuss with them how it might be possible to avoid excessive pressure. Remarks like "You don't have to be so careful with this project, the customer is already perfectly satisfied," don't usually come across very well. From the Type 1 point of view, we always deliver high quality because it is important to us. More

effective might be a reduction of the number of tasks a Type 1 has to handle, and giving him responsibility for projects where very high quality is an issue.

• Be careful how you offer criticism. Type 1 is already quite hard on himself. It can be painful when his environment points out areas for improvement that he hadn't noticed himself. Criticism is easier to accept when the people giving it include themselves, showing a certain amount of self-criticism as well. This makes it clear to the 1 that he is not the only one who could use some improvement. Appropriate humor can also be useful, allowing the 1 to keep things in proportion.

• Type 1 seldom sees the quality of his own work as sufficient. On the other hand, the 1 as client, boss or colleague is the first to pick up on quality issues. It is a worthwhile investment to deliver the highest possible quality to a 1.

Suggestions for development

• Make a list of projects for which you are responsible. Note down what degree of perfection your environment would find acceptable for them. Balance this against your own standards. Choose a project where you will let go of your own quality standards and not aim for a level higher than it needs to be. Evaluate the effects of your action when the project is completed.

• Ask your staff what they think of your management style. If they think you over-critical or quick to take offence, ask them what behavior they would find more supportive.

• Type 1 is good at criticizing himself and others. Try doing the opposite. Give yourself five compliments every day. Write down the compliments and look at them after a month. Don't let yourself be distracted by thoughts that the compliments are exaggerated or nonsensical.

• Type 1 rarely takes time to relax. It can be helpful to plan brief periods of relaxation. Make a list of ten activities or situations that relax you. Choose two that you are going to make time for within the next two weeks. Plan the time necessary in your diary and evaluate the results when the two weeks are up.

Type 2

The Helper

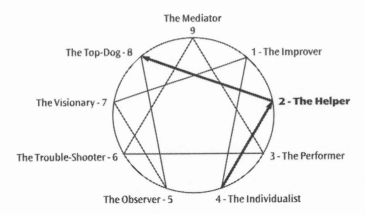

The Mediator
9

The Top-Dog - 8

1 - The Improver

The Visionary - 7

2 - The Helper

The Trouble-Shooter - 6

3 - The Performer

The Observer - 5

4 - The Individualist

Left behind in the supermarket, Type 2 thinks to himself

"You know what, I'm going to ask the woman on check-out if her shoulders are tense from all that repetitive work on the till. I can give her a massage, I'm sure she'd like that. Then I'll get her a cup of coffee while she has a break. Who knows, maybe she'll give me a lift home afterwards...."

What others appreciate in Type 2

- Genuine interest in others
- Masterly networker; knows how to win others' appreciation
- Senses precisely what others feel or need
- Good at supporting and motivating others
- Service-oriented; always there when needed

What others find difficult in Type 2

- Don't recognize their own needs
- Need a great deal of approval
- Put people before results
- Can be slightly intrusive
- Tend to think themselves indispensable, and are proud of it, too.

Type 2 national culture

- Thailand

Type 2 Self-assessment

"I've always been able to relate to people, ever since I was a child. My boss and I understand each other really well. I know he wouldn't be as successful as he is if I wasn't there to support him. He frequently discusses important decisions with me. Talking to me helps him to get further. The same is actually true of a lot of people in this company. My network is broad, and people often call on me to ask my advice. I hear a lot from my co-workers, as well as from my boss. It's not only about the company and their problems at work; they often talk to me about private matters, too. I take that for granted, because you can't really separate work and private life. So I'm used to other people telling me things. I don't understand how other managers can provide leadership without knowing what's going on for their staff. I always get involved with people; in fact, I think that is one of the best parts of my job. It's not only my colleagues and the boss who ask

me for advice. I coach various people I don't otherwise have any contact with on a daily basis. Even the Chairman of the Board regularly talks things over with me, although I don't report to him directly. It's something that just started happening over the years, and I'm glad to be involved. I don't often go to other people with my problems. I'll manage. I'm good at interpersonal relationships; always have been. I get a feeling for people quite quickly and I speak their language. That has its advantages in my work with clients. I think the company appreciates my ability to get on with everybody, and my helpfulness."

Issues for Type 2

• Being indispensable
Type 2 doesn't want to be in the limelight, but likes to be considered important. Indeed, the maintenance of an extensive network inside and outside the organization is one way in which the 2 makes himself indispensable.

"I'd wager a guess that I hold a key position in this company. People come to me with their problems because they feel understood. It's because I know so much about what is going on that the director often asks my advice about how he should handle others. I give him a bit of coaching in people management. He could have got himself into a few sticky situations if I hadn't been around. In that respect, he still has a lot to learn, but I can give him a hand."

• Own needs
The 2 is not quick to show when he needs help himself.

"Do I have to tell people to help me when they can see I'm up to my ears and they're not busy? In situations like that, you just help, that's obvious. I don't need to point it out. And if they don't even notice, then I'd rather do it myself anyway."

• Rapport and manipulation

Type 2 senses what others are feeling, what they want or need. It can be tempting for him to take advantage of this.

"When I walk into a meeting, I can sense immediately how everyone is feeling. One person needs a pat on the shoulder, someone else is dying for a coffee break, and another is keen to get into a critical discussion. Most people don't really notice these things, but I do. It makes it quite easy for me to be supportive. That way, I can always get them to do something for me, when I need it."

• Second fiddle

Type 2 may not want to be in the limelight personally, but he likes to be the power behind the throne. Surprisingly to others, this can put the brakes on his career development.

"I'm the vice-president here, and the position suits me perfectly. My boss treats me as a sparring partner and I am his most valuable advisor. I write a lot of his reports and accompany him to important meetings. He says I'm qualified to take over his position when he moves up. I don't know if I would want to do that. I think this role is more suitable for me."

• The importance of relationships

Good relationships with others are vital for the 2.

"I do this job because of the people. I believe we're productive. That is essential for survival in this business. My colleagues are always free to call me and drop by at the weekend if necessary. I consider many of my colleagues as my friends. I wouldn't know how else to work."

• Service orientation

Type 2 provides unparalleled service.

"Clients love me. I can understand that. I would do anything for them—well, practically anything. At home in San Francisco, I learned that good service means delivering more than the client expects. That appeals to me. I can settle complaints so well that clients are usually very impressed. That's how you build up a solid network."

Management style

The 2 generally prefers relationship-oriented leadership. The focus is on coaching and empowerment.

"The best part of my work is being a coach for my staff. I talk to them about their qualities and how they can put them to the best use. I see myself more as their friend and coach. I get a lot out of people that way."

Under pressure or stress: Shift to 8

Type 2 moves in the direction of Type 8 when under pressure or feeling stress. Some of Type 8 characteristics may then become apparent.

Stress can be caused by a lack of appreciation. This can lead to:
• Wounded pride;
• Anger and aggression.

"I'm always available for my boss, but recently, I don't hear a word of thanks for it. He can just go and sort himself out for a change."

Relaxed: Shift to 4

When relaxed, Type 2 moves in the direction of 4. The characteristics of Type 4 that may then appear are:
• Improved ability to recognize his own needs;
• Greater awareness of his own identity.

"It's not easy for me to focus on myself. But once I get to that point, I feel good about it. I do what I want to do, without my attention wandering off to others and what they need."

Type 2 Organizational characteristics

- Important place given to employee development
- The customer is king
- Service orientation
- Wants appreciation, but won't enforce it
- Problems within the organization may be overlooked
- People are more important than achievements
- Focus on leadership through coaching
- Employees allowed to voice their opinions.

How to get along with Type 2

- Approval is important for a 2, so don't be miserly with compliments. Of course, you have to mean it. A simple 'thank you' for a service the 2 has done for you is often sufficient.
- It can be tempting to take advantage of the almost intrusive helpfulness of the 2. It's as if they would polish your shoes for you if you asked them to. Don't be surprised if you sometimes feel slightly contemptuous of this behavior, but don't let yourself get carried away; think how it could be put to work effectively. This is a pattern that is more likely to appear in employees than in the role of manager.
- Ask explicitly what support the 2 needs, he won't usually volunteer the information.
- Show personal involvement.
- If you think a Type 2 needs something, don't wait for him to ask you for it.

Suggestions for development for Type 2

• Take stock of all the people in your organization that you have helped during the last year. Presumably they are your boss, your staff and some of your colleagues. Ask them where they found your support valuable and which situations they would rather not have had your involvement, or would have preferred you to help in a different way. If some people found you intrusive in certain situations, find out how this might be handled differently in the future.

• Make a list of five tasks you would like some help with, but are not likely to ask for. Select one and approach one of your colleagues, your boss or someone else with a request for support. Evaluate your experience of this afterwards.

• Examine which activities you do as a favor to someone else, rather than because you find them particularly important tasks. Drop the activity you find least important and develop another in its place that you find more meaningful.

• Experiment with showing yourself off a bit more. Think of a situation or project where you usually play second fiddle. Make a resolution to take the lead for a change. Evaluate the results afterwards.

TYPE 3

The Performer

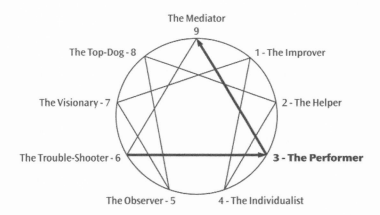

Left behind in the supermarket, Type 3 thinks

"I can figure out a way to make optimal use of my time. I can start by stocking the shelves. That's a nice little job, and others will notice my contribution..."

What others appreciate in Type 3

- High level of efficiency
- Goal orientation
- Ability to get things done
- Motivational effort
- Appropriateness.

What others find difficult in Type 3

- Competitiveness
- Sensitivity to status and image
- Opportunism
- Impatience with inefficiency
- Extreme self-confidence, bordering on arrogance.

Type 3 national culture

- U.S.A.

Type 3 Self-assessment

"I've always been a success at what I do. Not that I put a lot of effort into it, it usually just happens. I assume others see me as successful, and that's probably accurate. I really am quite good at some things. I'm successful at work, I have a wonderful wife and children, live in a nice house, drive a smart car and rank among the best in my profession, compared to most others of my generation. But it all mostly happened as a matter of course, probably because I enjoy my work. I put a lot into my job, and I work with competent people. I have had to learn to control my impatience. Some people can be so slow. I mean, I get along with people very well, with my staff for example. It's just that some of them need a little time before the penny drops. There are a few slowcoaches in my management team who try my patience at times too. Luckily, that's improving. I don't like failing, but happily, that seldom occurs. One way or another, I usually sense when

something has the potential for success. And if I do make a mistake, then we all learn something from it. My business unit books the highest achievements in the organization. We work hard for it. I used not to notice when things were moving too fast for one of the members of the team. I didn't pay attention to their feelings and they would feel overlooked. That has improved now. I think I'm appreciated here for my achievements and my enthusiasm for the job."

Issues for Type 3

• Efficiency

Fast results are important for Type 3. And he achieves them, when he's goal-oriented and able to work efficiently. The 3 is not easily angered or irritated unless someone or something hampers his efficiency. Bureaucratic organizations are difficult for a 3 and he probably won't feel comfortable in this kind of environment. However, the reality is that the world is not always as efficiently organized as the 3 would like it to be. Learning to deal with this dilemma is usually an issue for the 3.

"I get annoyed with colleagues who need more time to think before they can make a decision. 'Just do it,' I think to myself. Half a decision is better than none at all."

"I don't know what my colleagues want a lunch break for. I usually plan a lunch appointment with a client or one of my staff. Otherwise I just eat a sandwich while I'm working."

• Competition

The 3 likes to win, and that means having to compete sometimes. That doesn't imply that the 3 is a solo player. A team can also be a winner, and a team win means reflected glory for its individual members. Ordinary employees are allowed to score too, because when they score, their boss also wins. When the drive to compete is combined with the urge for opportunistic gain, the 3 can get everyone moving.

"In our department, I started a scheme whereby the employee who sold most in the course of a month won a bottle of champagne. It's no big deal, but it is fun, and I think everyone feels the same way about that."

• Profile
Type 3 enjoys working hard, but it is important that his environment acknowledges the results. Projects that don't pay off are less interesting. A boss who claims the credit for a 3's successes is no good.

"I see nothing wrong in getting publicity. Certainly not when it helps achieve more acceptance for the project we're working on. I think it's a good thing for my staff to let it be known what they're doing. The entire department benefits. But I have also had the experience of my previous boss using my achievements to make himself look good, without mentioning my name. That made me furious."

• Failure
The self-image of a Type 3 is largely defined by the successes he books. Failure damages the self-image and is to be avoided. The 3 has a good sense of the win or lose potential of a project, thus is good at avoiding failure. Failure in conjunction with a loss of face can be extremely difficult for him.

"I've been out of operation for the last three months because of illness. Naturally, that can happen to anyone, but I still had the feeling that I had to find excuses. I'm never sick. People could have imagined all sorts of things."

• Feelings

Feelings of insecurity, doubt and anxiety don't really belong to the 3's self-image. He doesn't talk about such things much and is not always very patient with others when they feel low. If you have to have feelings, then have them preferably after working hours. You can postpone feelings until later.

"Of course I have doubts about my work sometimes too. And I had some serious personal matters to deal with recently. But there's no point in letting myself get distracted during working hours. I'm quite good at more or less postponing my feelings of discomfort. I might feel lonely or sad sometimes when I'm off work. My tendency then is to keep myself busy, but I have also learned that it's good to give myself time to see it through."

• Image and status

The achievement of status and maintaining a good image are not negligible matters for the 3.

"I don't show off, that's not done in a country like The Netherlands. But if I'm asked, I see no reason to hide where I live and what kind of car I drive. I've made an excellent name for myself over the years and it makes me feel good to realize that. I also enjoy working for a company with such an excellent reputation in our field."

Management style

The 3 is task-oriented and inclined to reward competence.

"I know how to achieve results, and that helps to attract people to work for me. If they do well, I give them plenty of opportunities, and they appreciate that. They can always count on me and I will also encourage them, as long as they keep up the good work."

Under pressure or stress: Shift to 9

Type 3 moves to 9 when under pressure or feeling stress. Some of Type 9 characteristics that may then become apparent are:
• Losing the overview, getting tied up in details;
• Shutting down, not being assertive.

"I normally know exactly what I'm doing and I make it perfectly clear. I'm not in the right place in this team. I can't get going. I'm quieter and say less. I don't recognize myself. It's not a comfortable position to be in."

Relaxed: Shift to 6

Type 3 moves to 6 when he feels comfortable. The characteristics of Type 6 that may then manifest:
• More attention given to feelings and doubts;
• More time for reflection.

As a rule, recognition of the state of relaxation leads to more integration.

"Some years ago I was invited to talk about my possible role in a highly reputed organization as consultant during an important change process. I was flattered that they thought of me. Towards the end of my discussion with the Human Resources director of the company, he asked me what might go wrong with my method of coaching, if I should be asked to lead the project. The question threw me off balance to a certain extent. I explained to him how smoothly matters would be organized if I got the job. In the end the contract was given to someone else. When I enquired why, it turned out that the client didn't feel comfortable with a consultant who didn't seem to know his own limits. Of course I had my doubts about certain matters, but during a discussion like that they simply don't arise. When I'm sitting at home with my wife, it's easier for me to see what my own feelings are about this. I'm starting to be able to see my doubts and

feelings when they arise in work now, too. Those around me tell me they appreciate this in me. They say I'm less of a superman; a bit more human."

Type 3 Organizational characteristics

- Efficient
- Hard-working
- Internal competition
- More focus on results than on people
- High remuneration, linked to performance
- Only winners are shown appreciation
- Importance of good image
- Short-term results are essential.

How to get along with Type 3

- Speak more in terms of opportunities and solutions than of risks and problems.
- The 3 are more interested in concrete results than fine words.
- If there is any question of opposing interests, suggest solutions with benefits for all parties.
- Don't be unsettled by the 3's boundless self-assuredness. When the 3 is alone, he has doubts too.
- The 3 likes his performance to be acknowledged. But of course, this only works if you really do appreciate his achievements.

Suggestions for development for Type 3

- Put together a mild 'slow-down' program for yourself with ten possible action points. Choose two to three items that you are going to put into practice. Evaluate the effect after a few weeks.
- Check whether and to what extent your staff feel overlooked by you, especially in situations they feel less competent to handle. Ask them what they would like to see changed.

• Review a situation in which you felt a little uncertain, but didn't let it be seen. Next time you find yourself in a situation like that, show a little of your uncertainty as well as your optimism. Examine the effect on yourself, on the situation and for the others involved.

• Make a note of what makes you feel irritated during the course of a week. Presumably these will be situations where matters have not been handled efficiently, you've been caught up in some form of bureaucracy, or you had to deal with incompetent people. How do you react? Perhaps you get angry with someone, or swallow your irritation, or you find that it drives you to work harder. Evaluate your reactions and make a resolution to experiment with a different way of handling a similar situation in the future.

TYPE 4

The Individualist

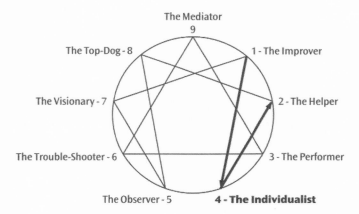

Left behind in the supermarket, Type 4 thinks

"At home, I used to long for a place of my own, without my mother. How wonderful, to be alone, scouting out the world. I thought it would be great. Now that I'm here, I'm not so sure. This is not real life either. I want to go home..."

What others appreciate in Type 4

- Sensitivity
- Aesthetic appreciation
- Deep interest in their own and others' feelings about things
- High degree of authenticity
- Contemplative.

What others find difficult in Type 4

- Wants to be different from everyone else
- Moody
- Unrealistic; wants the inaccessible
- Never really satisfied
- Overly emotional.

Type 4 national culture

- Italy

Type 4 Self-assessment

"I've always had a strong sense of self-awareness, ever since I was a little boy. I felt different from other people. I was more sensitive, more artistic. In retrospect, I felt that I was more authentic than most other people were. In a way, it was nice to be special, and I was totally in love with life. But it was also lonely. Sometimes I felt quite melancholy. Then life seemed gray and I longed for more color, more intensity, more feelings. I despised other people's bourgeois lives, but it also occurred to me that it might be pleasant to be able to feel contented with home, hearth and family. My moods are usually less extreme now, but I still feel intensely irritated if people don't understand me, or quite ecstatic when I experience something really beautiful. Luckily I'm able to be myself at work and don't need to hold myself back very much. The fact that I express my emotions is precisely what people appreciate, and also that I find it important to do meaningful work. People feel safe to

express their own emotions with me, because they know I experience them too. I encourage my staff to be themselves and to talk more about what is really on their minds. Some people want to work for me precisely for that reason. Of course, there are a lot of little gray mice around here too. But I can often get them to talk about themselves. And as long as I can express my feeling for aesthetics and creativity in my own way, I'll go on working here. That's what I like about the attitude in this company."

Issues for Type 4

• Moods

Moods can be overwhelming, although the job situation can also be used to moderate them.

"The weather, music, my clothes, the dreams I've had—everything influences my mood. Being at the office has the effect of dampening my mood, and sometimes that is just as well."

• Emotional depth

Type 4 likes to talk about the fundamentals of life, not about superficialities.

"I wouldn't say that I don't like my job, but I do it out of financial necessity. I rarely meet interesting people at work. When the conversation takes a turn towards something interesting once in a while and I ask a more personal question, most of my colleagues and clients look a bit startled."

• Sensitivity

Type 4 is sensitive to what is going on inside himself.

"I realize now, of course, that it's not always appropriate to rhapsodize over the beautiful patterns the sun is making on the wall, while I'm in a

meeting with an important client. But that doesn't mean that I'm not experiencing the emotion."

• Authenticity
It's important to be able to be yourself, and to be in surroundings where others also have that freedom.

"Let's be honest, most of the people around here are boring. I'm often the only one who shakes things up a bit. Some people enjoy that, others think I'm acting up."

• Misunderstood and unique
The 4 is often aware of his uniqueness, which also accounts for feeling misunderstood.

"I'm not the same as most of the others around here. I'm more sensitive, deeper. It's enjoyable, but it's also lonely. They say they like me working here precisely because I'm different. I'm not convinced. Perhaps I should work for myself, I find that quite an attractive idea sometimes."

• Greener grass
Type 4 has a tendency to keeping looking elsewhere, because of the feeling that more is to be attained somewhere other than where they are.

"It sometimes seems as if other people are able to find the happiness I'm looking for. That makes me wonder what they have that I haven't got. I feel a bit jealous at times. I used to keep searching for something. I remember how I used to long for a partner. Then when I had a lover, I longed for freedom. I realize now that it usually has more to do with me than with my circumstances."

Management style

Type 4 gives a lot of individual attention to staff members and is very tolerant of their feelings. He stimulates people to be themselves and encourages everyone to express their own unique talents.

"I'm the kind who is there when people need me. They can talk to me, and I give them the depth they need. I rely on everyone knowing for themselves how best they can develop their own talents."

Under pressure or stress: Shift to 2

Type 4 moves to 2 when under pressure or feeling stress.
Some of Type 2 characteristics that may then become apparent are:
• Attention diverted to others; less in contact with his own feelings;
• Minimizes his own originality and authenticity in order to win more approval.

"In my previous job I was increasingly oriented towards what others expected of me. I wore the clothes that went with my position and repressed my idiosyncrasies. In appraisals I was told that I was easier to get along with, but inside I knew I was selling myself short. I realized I was fitting in mostly because it didn't feel safe to be who I really was."

Relaxed: Shift to 1

Type 4 moves to 1 when he is relaxed.
Some Type 1 characteristics that may then appear:
• A more systematic approach to work and life;
• Delivers perfect quality and is less subject to moodiness.

"When I'm in good form, I create excellence of the highest standard that also has a lot of myself in it. I'm less subject to moods and feel connected to the world around me."

Type 4 Organizational characteristics

• Primary accent on exclusiveness
• Products must be beautiful; aesthetics are important
• Highly creative
• Strongly emotional
• Little teamwork
• Staff win appreciate through individual contributions
• Resistance to business-like attitude; would rather be exclusive than big
• Preference for a few special clients rather than many average clients.

How to get along with Type 4

• The 4 will pay more attention to you if he sees that you have something to say about your own inner feelings and the fundamental aspects of life and work.
• Make sure that the 4 has a position where his creativity can be fully utilized. Minimize formalities and standard procedures.
• It's important for the 4 to be able to do things in his own way.
• It is unnecessary to get upset about the 4's intensive emotionality. Don't try to find solutions, but don't run away from them either.
• Be yourself. Of course, that's always important, but it is especially so with a 4. He sees through feigned emotion and it won't win his respect.

Suggestions for development for Type 4

• Take note of the situations with staff, clients and colleagues where you feel the need to talk more about real feelings and meaningful matters for the next week. Investigate a few of these situations to see what attitude the others involved would have had if you had asked more questions. In the situations where you did, in fact, take matters further, enquire how the others involved felt about it. Evaluate your findings and see what conclusions you come to.

• Make a list of ten things you could either do or refrain from doing that would allow you to feel more yourself. Choose two to experiment with for a few months. This could entail a shift of emphasis in your dealings with some people, or an apparently unimportant change, such as hanging up your favorite painting in your office.

• Ask your colleagues to what extent they find you too intense. Find out what it is that bothers them and what you would need to change in your behavior to put them more at ease. Ask them what they like about your intensity.

• Do some research into your moods. If you notice a difference between your moods at home and at work, examine what it is that makes the difference, and in which situations you feel more comfortable. See what there is in one situation that teaches you something about another.

TYPE 5

The Observer

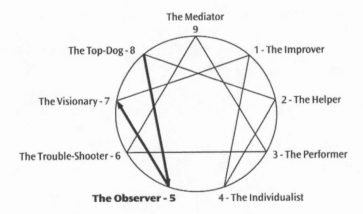

The Mediator
9

The Top-Dog - 8

1 - The Improver

The Visionary - 7

2 - The Helper

The Trouble-Shooter - 6

3 - The Performer

The Observer - 5

4 - The Individualist

Left behind in the supermarket, Type 5 thinks

"I think I'll go and sit behind one of the shelves. I'll be out of sight, but I can still see what's going on. I'll be able to see who buys which products, and when. Perhaps I'll discover an underlying pattern in shopping behavior…"

What others appreciate in Type 5

• Knowledge about different things

- Analytic ability
- Systematic approach
- Relativist
- Fast decision-maker when the information is available.

What others find difficult in Type 5

- Emotional distance
- Strict separation of work and private life
- Indirect reaction to matters outside his field of expertise
- Resistance to spontaneity
- Selectively sympathetic.

Type 5 national culture

- England

Type 5 Self-assessment

"I've always had an ability for precise analysis. I was like that as a child. I like to observe and analyze. Actually, it just happens. Whether I have to make a strategic choice, or talk to one of my staff, the process is basically the same. I observe, analyze and decide. It doesn't take a lot of effort and I'm pretty quick. Provided I have all the necessary information. Others find me somewhat distant and withdrawn. Some think I lack emotion. The latter is certainly not true, but I admit that I had to learn to show my feelings more, and it's not something I'm fond of doing. My natural tendency is not to let more of myself be seen than is strictly necessary. I like my privacy. I appreciate my colleagues and staff very much, but I prefer them not to disturb me too often when I'm at home. You have to draw boundaries. I'm good at acquiring knowledge; it comes easily to me. I gather the necessary information and then I know where I'm going. I like written communication. It gives me the opportunity to reflect and let things sink in. I often ask for time to think in meetings and I find it useful

to be able to read up beforehand on the matters under discussion. My expertise and my ability to oversee wide-ranging projects are what earn me appreciation in this company."

Issues for Type 5

• Privacy

Privacy is important to the 5, and the need for it can manifest in various ways.

"I have finally decided to have a mobile phone in the car, but only my secretary and my wife know the number. I've made sure that my number is not in the internal telephone book. I drive a lot, and time at the wheel is valuable to me, because it gives me the opportunity to think things over."

• Personal space

Some Type 5s must have their own private room to be able to function well. Others are good at creating their own private space, even in the presence of others.

"When our company relocated recently, it had considerable consequences for the office allocation. In the old building, each consultant had heir own room, but we had to share with someone else in the new one. The argument for this was that as consultants, we spend most of our time out with clients anyway. I couldn't accept that. I'm with other people most of the day and I need time for myself where I can work undisturbed. Other than the director, I'm the only person who has his own office. If that hadn't been possible, I don't know if I would have stayed with the company."

"I don't mind whether I have a room to myself or have to share with others. I can close myself off completely and don't even notice whether the others are there. My colleagues find that difficult sometimes, because apparently I don't always answer when they ask me something."

• Knowledge
The acquisition of knowledge is easy and interesting for the 5.

"I've just started a new job. It was only a matter of weeks before I was up to speed. I read a few books and then I'm able to hold my own quite quickly."

• Recharging batteries
It's interesting to be with other people, but it can be tiring. We charge our batteries when we're alone.

"I go for a walk for half an hour after work. It replenishes me."

"I take a long weekend to go away somewhere on a regular basis. I like to go off on my own and then I'm fully recharged when I come back."

• Decision-making
It is easy to make a decision in one's area of expertise, once sufficient information has been gathered.

"I think a lot of my colleagues work harder than I do. I find 40 hours a week quite enough, and I usually manage to do what is necessary in that time. My approach is relatively simple. I have my staff write me memos about the important matters, I read their conclusions and then make my decision."

• Reflection
Type 5 takes plenty of time for reflection, and may consider reviewing and thinking ahead as the most important parts of his experience.

"Sometimes I seem to take three times the time others need to do something. When I have a meeting, I want to be able to think about how it may

go and what subjects will be discussed beforehand. Then there is the meeting itself. Then afterwards I have to review what happened."

"To be honest, I often find the post-mortem after a party more interesting than the party itself."

Management style
Task-oriented management is usually easy for a 5. Relationship coaching is often an issue.

"I had to learn how to be a leader. My staff usually considered that I took care of everything, but they found me too distant. I did some courses and learned to keep my door open for them. It didn't really help. The staff said that although I left my door open, I erected an invisible barrier in its place. One saying "Do not disturb." Now I make appointments to see them and I've introduced a fixed period when they can walk in unannounced. Perhaps it's a bit artificial, but it works."

Under pressure or stress: Shift to 7

Type 5 moves to 7 when under pressure or feeling stress.
Some of Type 7 characteristics that may then become apparent are:
• Abundant thoughts and ideas, without any of them being taken further;
• Humor used as a protective device.

"The last time I went to the company's New Year party, I was bombarded with questions about a complicated personal situation I was in at the time. I used a good dose of humor to combat what was, in my view, inappropriate curiosity. Later I heard that a lot of people thought I was unusually outgoing. For me, it was an unpleasant situation that humor enabled me to get through."

At ease: Shift to 8

Type 5 moves to 8 when he is relaxed.
Some Type 8 characteristics that may then appear:
• Less thinking, more direct exchange;
• Feelings more on the surface.

"I feel more energetic when I'm at ease, and I express myself more clearly. "

Type 5 Organizational characteristics
• Considerable expertise
• Oriented towards long-term results
• Not highly commercial
• Functional contacts between colleagues
• Clear separation of business and personal matters
• Average people management
• Good internal organization
• Achieves success as a center of excellence.

How to get along with Type 5

• A 5 doesn't vaunt his expertise, but is quite ready to share it on request. Don't wait for it to come to you; ask what you want to know explicitly.

• The 5 needs time to decide what his own standpoint is. He can come to a fast decision when he has collected sufficient information. If you want to speed up his decision-making process, give him plenty of written information beforehand. He'll have done most of his analysis before the meeting even takes place.

• Spontaneous mini-meetings are not the 5s strong point. It usually works better to make an appointment. Rather than asking "Hey, what did you think of the report" when you bump into him at the coffee-machine, try asking "Can I drop in to see you for 5 minutes around midday to hear your opinions about the report?"

• The 5 is good at written communication. Where you might be inclined to give a quick phone-call to someone else, a fax or email could be a good alternative for a 5.

• If the 5 doesn't express his appreciation, that doesn't automatically mean that he's dissatisfied. If he were dissatisfied, he would either have said something or simply not given you any of his time.

Suggestions for development for Type 5

• Make a point of using verbal communication instead of writing. Choose five items where you would normally write a memo, shoot off an email or fax, and for the space of a week, go to see the person or phone them instead. Enquire of yourself, as well as the other person, how your approach is experienced. On the basis of your analysis, see if there is anything that you would like to change in your method of communicating.

• At two meetings you have to attend, make an effort to contribute more to the discussion of subjects that don't fall into your own area of expertise. You might do this by asking more questions, or offering succinct summaries. Evaluate your findings.

• For a period of two weeks, make more contact with your staff than usual. Be more insistent on finding out how they are. If you really plan to do this, it could be useful to let your staff know in advance. That way, you won't take them by surprise and they will be more supportive of your initiative.

• Ask your staff what they think of your style of management, particularly with regard to your emotional involvement. If they see this as an issue for you, ask them what they would find more supportive.

TYPE 6

The Trouble-Shooter

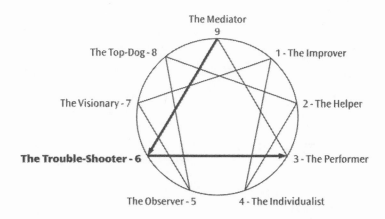

The Mediator
9

The Top-Dog - 8

1 - The Improver

The Visionary - 7

2 - The Helper

The Trouble-Shooter - 6

3 - The Performer

The Observer - 5

4 - The Individualist

Left behind in the supermarket, Type 6 thinks:

"This mustn't be allowed to happen again. Next time Mom wants to go out, I'll ask her where she's going. If we're going to the supermarket, I'll ask her what she's going to buy and how long it will take. Then I'll hold on to

her hand and won't let go until we're home again. If she does let go of my hand I'll scream so loudly, she'll just have to pay attention…"

What others appreciate in Type 6:

- Critical questioning
- Proactive thinking
- Involvement with people
- Loyalty
- Courage in discussing difficult matters.

What others find difficult in Type 6:

- Cautious scenarios
- "Yes, but" comments
- Ambivalence
- Doubting their own success and that of others
- Need for too much information.

Type 6 national culture:

- Germany

Type 6 Self-assessment

"I've always felt a need for certainty about things. As a child, I thought it was better to be safe than sorry, and I still think that. I'm good at identifying potential dangers and being ready to meet them. I don't find it easy to formulate scenarios that extend over a period of years. Others think my prognoses are a bit on the cautious side, but I know that we haven't overlooked many serious threats, so reality can only turn out to be better than expected. I like to bring difficult matters out into the open. It might have to do with abuse of authority or a proposal for a project that a colleague hasn't thought through properly. I find it easy to ask critical questions. That might be interpreted as opposition to the proposal on my part, but that's

not necessarily the case. I'm more interested in examining whether the argumentation is correct, in order to achieve better results. If I feel unsafe or threatened, I may crawl back into my shell to consider what I should do. On other occasions I lash out, when attack seems to be the best means of defense. That can come across as being very powerful, even though I feel unsure of myself. Success is nice of course, but it can also make me feel uncomfortable. Success makes you prone to criticism from others, and what looks like success today might turn out to be a fiasco tomorrow. I value clear agreements and rules, and reliable friendships. It all helps achieve clarity in your life. Some people find me a bit ambivalent, and that is true occasionally. What's true today could change tomorrow. The world changes so quickly. That's why I don't always find it easy to make a deci-sion. I like to stand up for the weaker ones, not just in the office, but at home, too. This company values me for my reliable efforts, my involvement with people and my ability to think strategically."

Issues for Type 6

• Loyalty
Being loyal is second nature to the 6.

"I've given a lot to this company for years. I sometimes ask myself why. It was more for the others than for myself. And I don't regret that, but I've had enough of it now."

• Ambivalence
The problem with ambivalence is that it can hinder action.

"How do I know whether the new strategy is the right way to go? What was true on the basis of yesterday's facts isn't necessarily appropriate according to today's information."

• Attack is the best defense

Uncertainty may cause the 6 to withdraw, but it can also have the opposite effect of causing him to come forward courageously and openly.

"Sometimes I think I'm the only one who realizes the threat imposed by this management. I can't see any other option than to confront them with everything. I don't like it, but somebody has to do it."

• Standing up for the underdog
The 6 finds it easy to identify with the underdog.

"There are people in this company, especially those further down the ladder, who are not really having an easy time. I think we should take care of them better."

• Good analysis
The 6 can think ahead and is good at analysis.

"I'm often asked to review future scenarios. I'm good at it. I can see what might happen years ahead and can spot the possible threats."

• Hidden agenda
The 6 instinctively recognizes a hidden agenda and other things that could create uncertainty.

"Openness is important to me. I have a gut feeling for when someone is holding something back. Hidden agendas unsettle me, but I know how to bring them into the open."

Management style

Management is based on trust and security.

"I work on the basis that my staff is going to keep me informed of whatever is relevant. That concerns their work, but also anything that has to do with our way of working together. I respect them and I keep to the agreements I make with them. I'm critical in a constructive way. I had to learn how not to give in to my own doubts and ask critical questions all the time."

Under pressure or stress: Shift to 3

Type 6 may move to 3 when under pressure or feeling stress.
Some of Type 3 characteristics that may then become apparent are:
• Action rather than thought;
• Behavior that conforms to his surroundings, but not to his own self-image.

"Partly because of a major reorganization, my workload became too heavy for me. Loyal as I am, I worked even harder. I couldn't stop. My boss liked my new style of working, he thought I was more productive. By the end of two years I was showing quite a few signs of burn-out. I realized that my high productivity was mostly due to the high level of adrenaline that was pumping through my body all the time."

At ease: Shift to 9

Type 6 moves to 9 when he is relaxed.
Some Type 9 characteristics that may then appear:
• Less suspicious, more relaxed;
• Greater involvement with others.

"I feel like a different man when I'm relaxed. People find me easier to get along with and more tolerant. I think that's true."

Type 6 Organizational characteristics

- Bureaucratic
- Strict hierarchy
- Loyalty is highly valued
- Friendships used to strengthen internal network
- Members of the 'club' look out for each other
- Safety within; the danger comes from outside
- Good at developing future scenarios and strategies
- Entrepreneurship means taking calculated risks
- Long-term success is more important than quick fixes.

How to get along with Type 6

• The 6 likes to be kept informed. Matters that could seem trivial to others may be important for a six, so give the 6 as much information as possible.

• The 6 may appear to be in opposition, without believing in it himself. He's usually playing devil's advocate. Rather than resisting his perspective, it could be more useful to work with him to discover the truth.

• Type 6 is an unusually loyal employee. If his loyalty appears to be shaken, take it seriously. You may have lost his trust, or caused the 6 to feel insecure in some way.

• A 6 can be a difficult client. Make sure your proposals are well founded and that all the details have been thoroughly checked. Once you win his trust, a lot is possible.

• Be honest and open with the 6. He is allergic to hidden agendas and spots them immediately. He will appreciate openness.

Suggestions for development for Type 6

• Make a list of five dangers or risks you perceive for your team or company. Verify your assumptions as much as possible against the facts and the opinion of people whose judgment you trust. Examine which of the risks you saw were realistic and which of them may have been a little over the top. Consider what consequences your findings could have on how you deal with perceived threats in the future.

• Find out from your colleagues when your sometimes overly critical questions are useful and when they may be experienced as destructive. See how this could lead to an adjustment of your behavior in certain situations. Let your colleagues know about your intention and check with them after three months whether they have noticed any change.

• Ask your staff what they think would be the best way to keep you informed. Compare this with your own wishes. If your staff prefer less detailed reporting, see if you can come to an agreement with them and experiment with the new method for a few weeks. Evaluate the results. Was it possible to manage well with less information, or did it cause difficulties?

• Investigate loyalty with your employer. Take stock of situations during the last three years where you put great effort into work which you didn't think really useful or necessary, but which you did out of loyalty to your manager or employer. Consider which situations you would now handle in the same way, and which you would approach differently. Use your insight next time a similar situation arises.

TYPE 7

The Visionary

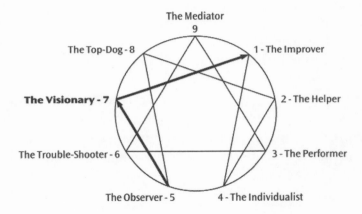

The Mediator
9

The Top-Dog - 8

1 - The Improver

The Visionary - 7

2 - The Helper

The Trouble-Shooter - 6

3 - The Performer

The Observer - 5

4 - The Individualist

Left behind in the supermarket, Type 7 thinks

"I'm enjoying myself. I can see all the chips, soft drinks and chocolate from here. It might be fun to try out some of the new brands. It's interesting to see who comes in here. I'd love to talk to all of them. I'm sure they all have fascinating hobbies. Maybe there's someone who does parachute jumps. I could go along too."

What others appreciate in Type 7

- Enthusiasm
- Charm and liveliness
- Always spots opportunities and refreshing aspects
- Full of inspiring ideas
- Knows how to enjoy life.

What others find difficult in Type 7

- Doesn't always finish what he starts
- Breaks agreements occasionally
- Easily bored
- Can seem superficial
- Avoids conflict.

Type 7 national culture

- Ireland

Type 7 Self-assessment

"I've always known how to have fun. I get hundreds of ideas for enter-taining and fascinating projects. I'm easily attracted to new things. However, once I know how things work, my attention shifts to another project or a new idea. Finishing things is not my strongest point, but I'm good at getting projects going. I find it easy to interest my staff, colleagues and clients in a concept I've thought up. I like to think up new concepts and always have more ideas than I have time to carry them all out. I'd rather not have to face conflict and painful matters. I used not even to notice their existence, but I've become more aware of them now. Others find me a bit superficial and perhaps childish. That's not true, but I am someone who likes to look on the bright side, and discover the possibilities of developing things in a positive way. I like variety, and that's apparent in my life. I have a lot of interests and hobbies. I think I've held more different positions in

my working life than many others have. I'm not an expert on anything, you might say I'm a Jack-of-all-trades. Freedom is important to me. Anyone who wants to boss me around is barking up the wrong tree. So long as someone understands that, we can get along. I think I'm appreciated in this company because of my enthusiasm and the ability to convey it to others, and for my abundance of ideas and creativity."

Issues for Type 7

• Rules and supervision
The 7 wants to be free. Rules can get in the way.

"It's ok to follow the rules when they make sense, but that's not the case with most rules." Having tasks supervised can also be experienced as restrictive. *"I decide for myself what time I start work, when I leave and what I do. If I'm sitting at home on a Sunday afternoon working on a great new idea, nobody has to sit there and supervise me."*

• Commitment and completion
The 7 likes to keep his options wide open. Commitment doesn't exactly fit that approach.

"When I first started to work as a Project Manager, I would occasionally leave a project before it was completed. I'd find I'd had enough of it, and there were so many other interesting possibilities to pursue. But it was disappointing for my project teams. I've found another way to handle that now. I only start a project when I already have my successor at hand. Then I can get out when I want to, without affecting the project or causing others disappointment."

• Variety
Driven by his enthusiasm and interest, the 7 seeks variety.

"A week-long on-site project with a customer is more than enough. By then I know the company, the people and everything they serve in the canteen. In short, it's time to move on."

"In the seventeen years I've been working, I've had fifteen different jobs and worked for six different companies. I enjoy variety and continuing to learn."

• Ideas and concepts

Type 7 has more than enough ideas that could be developed. Unfortunately, he never has the time for them. It's pleasant to have a big staff who can work on a number of different concepts, so that there is always time to make new plans.

"Name me a subject and I'll give you several good ideas to develop."

• Enthusiasm

Type 7 sees all the possibilities and is quickly enthused. This can be very stimulating for his environment.

"When staff members come to me with certain problems, I can always immediately see how to turn an apparent crisis into an interesting opportunity. I find it easy; it's second nature to me. I understand from my staff that they mostly find that this helps them to pick up the threads again. I think it's a wonderful way to work."

• Avoidance of conflict

The 7 is a master of finding creative ways to get around conflicts or put them in perspective.

"I think this project is going very well. Yes, there were some difficulties and problems with delivery, but what do you expect? It was a huge project.

So I feel very positive about it and I think that the client is finding more fault than necessary."

Management style

Freedom, giving people space and stimulating them, is the important aspects of management for a 7.

"I don't lean on my staff or look over their shoulders all the time. And if they do get in a mess, they have to figure out the solution for themselves. They are adults, after all. I give them a lot of freedom, and they appreciate that. Sometimes they think I don't give them enough attention, that I'm not around often enough. I've had to learn to be more structured and to build in time to talk to them. Otherwise some of them miss out. What I like most about management is not the power—that doesn't interest me greatly—but the freedom. I'm the boss of my own division, so nobody can tell me what I should do and when I should do it. The only person who has any say about my schedule is the Chairman of he Board. Apart from that, I like getting my staff enthusiastic about what we're doing. I'm good at that. I listen to their problems and always have plenty of ideas about how they should deal with them."

Under pressure or stress: Shift to 1

Type 7 moves to 1 when under pressure or feeling stress.
Some of Type 1 characteristics that may then become apparent are:
• Rigidity; convinced he's in the right;
• Importance given to detail.

"It's not often that I fail to imbue my staff or colleagues with enthusiasm for my plans, and that's just as well, because I can be a bit peevish if they won't go along with me. I have the tendency to go into great detail to convince them that I'm in the right. I can be very stubborn about that."

"When things get difficult for the company—and that has happened a few times during the last ten years, unfortunately—I have a tendency to make futile rules. I demand that everyone is in before nine, for example, that they turn in their worksheets on time and clear their desks before they leave. When things start getting better again, I usually forget about the rules again."

At ease: Shift to 5

Type 7 moves to 5 when he is relaxed.

Some Type 5 characteristics that may then appear:

• Accepts a limited number of projects, completes them thoroughly;

• Takes more time to think and is less vulnerable to apparently fascinating distractions.

"I'm quite different when I'm on vacation. I can spend a week sitting on a riverbank, painting. I need nothing and I'm totally contented."

Type 7 Organizational characteristics

• Minimal rules. New rules are resisted or ignored

• Difficulty with internal administration. "They just don't turn in their reports."

• Abundance of ideas

• Many unfinished projects

• Enthusiastic, youthful atmosphere

• Little respect for authority; respect must be won by charisma

• Can make large profits, but the overheads are too high

• Strong informal circuits; a lot is dealt with in the corridors and in the course of a weekend's outing

• Clients do not always take the company seriously. "They're pleasant people, full of enthusiasm, but they don't understand our real problems. Those we take to a different supplier."

• Unplanned ideas and activities are often a source of success.

How to get along with Type 7

• Make clear contracts, both verbally and in writing. The 7 has a more flexible attitude to contracts that the rest of the world.

• The 7 likes everything to be pleasant, and that means there is no room for conflict. They'll disappear like snow in sunshine at the first hint of it. If you really need to discuss a problem with a 7, don't be distracted by his charm and enthusiasm. It might help to try to formulate the problem more positively. More in the line of: "I think our co-operation presents an interesting challenge for both of us, " rather than "I have a bone to pick with you."

• Include the 7 whenever it's time for a brainstorming session or creative input.

• It's often easier to lure the 7 with a casual chat over a meal than a 'boring' meeting at work.

• If a 7's agreements with you are not adhered to, it is seldom because of who you are. The 7 just had other things to do. Don't take it too personally.

Suggestions for development for Type 7

• Discuss your management style with your staff. Ask them particularly about things like daily involvement and availability for meetings. Ask them for suggestions for improvement and make a selection of a few of them. Try them out for a period of four weeks and evaluate the effects.

• Make a list of your unfinished ideas or projects during the last two years. Indicate against each item to what extent it was right that it was abandoned, or to what extent they represent missed opportunities. Choose one idea that you intend to implement.

• Think about how many rules and regulations or meetings you managed to get around during the last year in your company. Look at the positive and negative effects they had on you and those around you. Develop your own conclusions about the different ways that you intend to deal with rules and meetings in the future.

• Ask your boss and other colleagues what conflicts or responsibilities they think you have overlooked because of your positive attitude. Choose one situation that you may not like, but which you are prepared to investigate further. Make a point of facing up to the conflict or the responsibility that was avoided. Evaluate the results.

TYPE 8

The Top-Dog

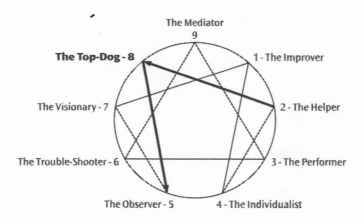

Left behind in the supermarket, Type 8 thinks

"I think we'll have to sort out this problem immediately. I'll tell that cashier she has to push me home in my pram straight away."

What others appreciate in Type 8

- Freedom of speech
- Stands up for his rights
- Stands by staff and friends
- Puts all his energy into doing the right thing
- Resistant to knocks.

What others find difficult in Type 8

- Not the most tactful
- Not always the best listener
- All or nothing approach
- Has difficulty letting go
- Tendency towards excessive behavior.

Type 8 national culture

- Spain
- Israel

Type 8 Self-assessment

"I've always known how to make it perfectly clear what I want. And I did it, too. In fact, I still do. You'd have to be really good to get me off track, especially when I know that the truth's on my side. I realize now, better than I used to, that my idea of the truth is not necessarily the same for everyone, and that it is good to listen to somebody else's point of view sometimes. I don't mind having a difference of opinion with other people. I think that's preferable to people keeping their mouths shut. At least a difference of opinion makes it clear where everyone stands. I respect those who maintain their opinion, although I have no inhibitions about letting them know exactly what I think about it. I have little respect for people who don't tell you their opinion, or go behind your back. They just don't count. I'm told I'm a bit too black-and-white in my thinking, and there may be some

truth in that. Someone is either acceptable or they're not. I'm not afraid of other people. Partly because I'm like that, I'm not always very tactful. Some say I talk out of turn and they think I'm a bit of an elephant in a china-shop. Luckily, that's less likely to happen these days."

"I've always found it difficult to see why people should be afraid of my straightforwardness. I don't mean ill with it. I can be very blunt to my staff sometimes, but if anyone else bothers them, they'll regret it, because they'll have me to deal with. I protect them as if they were my children. I like to blow up now and then. Why hold back when you can do the thing properly? I'm not very good at rules and bureaucracy. Life is like a highway. You're don't drive at 60 miles an hour just because the sign says you should, when the road is empty. I think I'm appreciated in this company because of my ability to get things done. I'm not afraid to get my hands dirty when necessary and I have the capacity to bring about considerable expansion."

Issues for Type 8

• Straightforwardness and tact

The 8 is very direct and outspoken. He speaks freely, seeing no reason to hoard opinions when it is also possible to share them. Tact, therefore, is not usually the 8's strongest point.

"I don't like to beat around the bush. If I don't like someone, I say so. If they're not happy with that, then they can just lay it out on the table and we'll soon see who's right. "

• Conflict and energy

The 8 finds conflict interesting. It clarifies everyone's position and is an enjoyable battle of wits.

"I like it when people argue with me. That doesn't mean that I give up easily. If the other person turns out to be stronger in the end, then I accept that. All the same, they won't forget me in a hurry."

The 8 is extremely energetic. Only old age or serious physical or psychic damage can slow him down.

"In the final analysis, I win most conflicts because of my tenacity. I simply keep going longer than most of my opponents."

• Listening

Listening properly is an issue for the 8. His argument is that there's usually not much to listen to.

"I don't steamroller over other people. They usually lie down as soon as I enter the room."

• All or nothing

The 8 considers others to be either interesting to talk to, or negligible. Staff members or colleagues are either treated like kings or like slaves. This has little to do with competence, but is more likely to be based on strength or weakness.

"I've had to get rid of a few people again; they couldn't fight their way out of a paper-bag. They say they're up to much more, but that I don't give them room to operate."

• Daddy

Type 8 protects his staff and his friends.

"I look after my people as if they were my children. If one of my colleagues or bosses tries to give them a hard time, they'll regret it. They'll have me to deal with, and they know it."

"I sent all my staff a color printer for Christmas. There was no way I could get permission to do that, because they're not even allowed to take a pencil home with them. But I found a way to arrange it, which just goes to show that my staff are much better off than people who work for my colleagues in the other divisions."

• The sky's the limit

Rules are made to be broken. You go as fast as possible when you can and slow down when you have to, not because someone else has decided that 60 miles an hour is fast enough. Rules are annoying because they reduce your capacity to control things.

"My staff complain that there are too few rules here. I don't get it. Let people behave like the adults they are. The criticism was really that I'm the one to decide on the rules and then change them whenever I feel like it."

The 8 translates this into 'the bigger the better'.

"Of course I could give a party for 20 people. But I think it would be more fun with 100, and it's not as if I haven't room enough in my house."

Management style

The 8 manager can keep a lot of balls in the air at the same time.

"'I'm not afraid to get my hands dirty. Anyone who doesn't pull his or her weight has to go. Not everyone can keep up with my pace, unfortunately, but that's just the way it is. Staff used to be afraid of me. That rarely happens now. I've learned to be a better listener and adjust my pace sometimes. We all work hard, and I reward them well."

Under pressure or stress: Shift to 5

Type 8 moves to 5 when under pressure or feeling stress.
Some of Type 5 characteristics that may then become apparent are:
• Withdrawal;
• Lack of sympathy.

Stress is particularly evident where treachery is perceived.

"They stabbed me in the back. I didn't say much after that. I felt like a beaten dog. The others took it as a good sign that I was a bit quieter. Their mistake. It was the calm before the storm. I felt humiliated and was out for revenge."

At ease: Shift to 2

Type 8 moves to 2 when he is relaxed.
Some Type 2 characteristics that may then appear:
• Power is used less to enlarge own territory and more to help others develop: empowerment in its purest form.
• Improved listening skills and greater adaptation to his surroundings.

"I kept going until I was out of my depth and many people had lost their trust in me before I realized what was happening. I was like a 6-cylinder turbo engine run wild. If it looked as if I might have to reduce my speed because of slower vehicles in front of me, I'd run over them if necessary. I'm quieter now and more relaxed. I'm better at adjusting my pace to suit others. I'm a better listener and more able to retain my staff. I think they can show themselves to better advantage now."

Type 8 Organizational characteristics

• Few rules and regulations, but a lot of unwritten laws
• Impulsive management; ad hoc decisions, but flexible

- Charismatic or authoritarian leadership
- Good rewards for those who give their all to the company
- Open communication, verbal rather than in writing
- Conflict is permitted, but not without risk: the loser is out
- Expansion of power and territory are important drivers
- Not afraid to meet competition head on.

How to get along with Type 8

- Be open and straightforward with the 8.
- Don't avoid conflict. The 8 usually only really respects someone who stays to face the music when there is a difference of opinion.
- Don't confuse openness for invulnerability. The 8 has a big mouth, but a timid heart.
- Set clear boundaries. What other people see as limits are not necessarily seen as such by the 8.
- Don't be too quick to take anger or conflict personally. It's often a better sign than if the 8 doesn't take any notice of you.

Suggestions for development for Type 8

- Ask your staff's opinion of your listening skills. Get some specific information about the circumstances in which they think you walk all over them or don't let them finish what they're saying. Find out how they experience those situations and what effects they have. Draw your own conclusions from your investigations and choose a few situations where you can observe your own listening skills. Evaluate your findings.
- Find out from your boss or colleagues whether they have the impression that employees are sometimes afraid of you. If they confirm this, ask them what they think you could do about it.
- Take stock of the conflicts or confrontations you've had during the last three months with the people around you. Think about how you reacted and to what extent you consider your reaction to have been

effective. Discuss your findings with someone you trust and ask them for their understanding of your interpretation.

• Consider the extent to which you might be subject to a vicious circle of working harder, wanting more results, wanting more power, an increasingly hectic life. Ask your partner or a good friend for their view. Use this conversation to decide on two things you will change in the coming quarter. Look at the results after three months. If you discover that you did not, or only partly acted on your resolve, investigate what it was in you that kept you from doing so.

TYPE 9

The Mediator

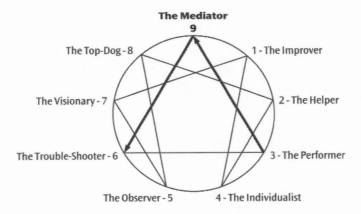

Left behind in the supermarket, Type 9 thinks

"Oh, I'll manage here alright, just as I always do. I have my toy car with me, I can play with that. It's nice and warm, just like home. The people are nice here too."

What others appreciate in Type 9:

- Ability to listen and understand others
- Willingness to compromise
- Acceptance of others
- Can narrow the gap between opposing views
- Flexibility in adapting to surroundings.

What others find difficult in Type 9:

- Avoids conflict
- Slow to take decisions
- Mediocre time management
- Lack of own opinion
- Indirect reactions when dissatisfied.

Type 9 national culture:

- The Netherlands
- Canada

Type 9 Self-assessment

"I've always found it easy to put myself in other people's shoes. I find it easy to understand people with an opposing viewpoint. There's something to be said for everything and all roads lead to Rome anyway. I'm not quick to express an opinion unless I'm asked for it. It's also difficult for me to stick to my guns. All the more because I often think it doesn't matter which route we choose. If I should happen to have a preference for something, I have no difficulty it letting it be known. But I don't like it if people don't listen to what I have to say, and then I won't budge from my point of view. People think I'm stubborn in that kind of situation. I like routine. It's often enjoyable and comfortable and you know where you are. And if it includes constructive habits as well, then there's nothing wrong with it. I'm a good intermediary when others have a conflict with each other. I'd rather avoid conflict myself

and prefer to keep the peace. I know this is not always a good thing, so I'm less inclined to ignore conflict now, but it still takes effort. Time management and setting priorities are not particularly easy for me. I'm easily distracted and I also think it's nice to be able to respond to whatever is happening in the moment. I'm appreciated in this company for my ability to create a good, supportive atmosphere in the teams I lead, and for my ability to bring people together, and my talent for people management."

Issues for Type 9

• Avoidance of conflict
Harmony is pleasant, conflict disturbs. Being able to understand others helps to avoid conflict. Facing conflict is demanding.

"I'm not quick to anger, but I can be erratic if I don't like a situation."

• Time management
Good time management is bothersome.

"How can you set priorities when there are so many important things to be done? I'm just about to start work on a strategic plan when one of my staff walks in and a client phones me. They're all equally important. So there's always a risk of things running late and having to be finished off at the last moment."

• Routine and distraction
The 9 likes comfortable habits and is easily distracted from himself or the essentials.

"I know I should write that report. But then I discover an interesting piece of research in my files that is relevant for my report. Naturally, I have to read it first."

• Mediating
The 9 understands many different points of view and is a good mediator.

"A very serious situation developed in our management team. A conflict got out of hand and a number of my colleagues wouldn't communicate with each other any longer. I seemed to be the only one that everyone still trusted and talked to about the situation."

• Decision-making and consensus
Decision-making can be difficult. First of all, it would be nice to arrive at a decision that everyone agrees with. That can take a long time, because everyone has to be brought into line. Sometimes we don't know what we want ourselves, and then it's easier to see what others want and go along with that. However, when the 9 finally realizes what he wants, he can be quite stubborn about getting it.

"It's not that I don't want to say what I want, I often simply don't know. There's something to be said for everything. When I finally know what it is I want—and that can take some time—I'm not shy about telling people. But then I find it difficult to face opposition. It's taken me long enough to formulate my own opinion; don't ask me to revise it all over again."

• Listening and taking a stand
It's easier for the 9 to listen to others than to take a stand himself.

"If a problem arises, I usually don't know what to think about it. I often need to hear others' opinions before I can figure out my own. By the time I'm ready to express my opinion, I often think it's all been said already, and then I don't bother saying anything."

Management style

The 9 creates a pleasant atmosphere with plenty of room for differences.

"I have a lot of time for my staff. They can talk to me, and I give them plenty of opportunity. I used to be accused of not standing up for them enough with management and other colleagues, so that they ended up getting the short end of the stick. That has improved now; I've got more backbone. My staff also used to think that I didn't let them know when things weren't going too well. They volunteered this information during their appraisals, without being asked. I try to be more straightforward now."

Under pressure or stress: Shift to 6

Type 9 moves to 6 when under pressure or feeling stress.
Some of Type 6 characteristics that may then become apparent are:
• Skepticism;
• Doubt.

"People used to be able to walk all over me. Eventually I'd get stubborn, verging on the suspicious. I wouldn't budge an inch from my position. That was my way of resisting them."

At ease: Shift to 3

Type 9 moves to 3 when he is relaxed.
Some Type 3 characteristics that may then appear:
• Action;
• Efficiency.

"I love my new job. I'm more results-oriented and I get a lot more done in less time."

Type 9 Organizational characteristics

• Consensus orientation
• Long processes and slow decision-making
• Unspoken, lingering conflicts

- Little apparent hierarchy
- Sociable
- Tolerant
- Attentiveness between employees
- Mediocre time management: meetings start late and run over time.

How to get along with Type 9

- Ask a lot of questions and listen properly—if only not to be taken by surprise by a standpoint that the 9 didn't air previously. "My supplier thought I'd given him the go-ahead, but later I realized I wasn't altogether satisfied with his proposal." The 9 is not quick to step into the limelight, but his opinion is relevant.
- If the 9 thinks it makes sense, it can be useful to offer support by providing structure.
- Take the time to create a pleasant atmosphere, talk about matters than may appear to be less essential.
- If the 9 is dawdling, it's usually an indirect way of exerting pressure. It usually helps to ask questions and give him some attention.
- The 9 is easily distracted by the wishes and plans of others. Don't ask too much of the 9, or make clear agreements with him.

Suggestions for development for Type 9

- Ask your staff whether they think that you avoid conflict with your colleagues and superiors. What are the situations where they think you are too easily influenced and don't protect their interests sufficiently, leading to a too heavy workload for them? Select two situations where you will be more straightforward in future. Evaluate the results afterwards.
- Find out from your boss the extent to which he thinks you defer decisions. What are the situations where you do this? What could you do or stop doing to help matters? Make a time-plan for a decision you

have to make and use the suggestions you have been given. Check back later to see what this achieved.

• Make a list of habits and unessential activities that occupy you each week. For two weeks, drop two of them each week. Evaluate your findings.

• Explore the process you went through during the last occasion when you had to convey bad news to someone. Did you postpone the discussion? Examine how the discussion went; how you felt during it and to what extent you were able to give your opinion clearly, and listen openly to the other person.

PART 2

ABOUT THE ENNEAGRAM

This section of the book deals with the most frequently asked questions about the Enneagram. The questions and answers are based on a selection of questions put to me during the course of work-shops I have led over the years. They demonstrate the most important questions that arise when managers and professionals first come into contact with the Enneagram.

The questions and answers are divided into four chapters. Chapter 1 contains questions relating to the Enneagram as a model. This includes information not yet touched upon, such as the history of the Enneagram and some subtleties of the model. A number of theories are discussed that help to explain the Enneagram in more detail.

Chapter 2 deals with questions about the use of the Enneagram in business. Considerable attention is given to answering questions about its use in management and project teams, and the risks associated with using the Enneagram within organizations. This chapter also discusses organizational typologies and the potential for changing them.

Working with the Enneagram, Chapter 3 looks at methods of implementing the Enneagram. This includes discussion of the typing interview and the panel.

Chapter 4 looks at questions concerning the relationship of the Enneagram to personal development. The Enneagram provides numerous links which managers and professionals may find helpful and supportive for their own personal development. This chapter offers suggestions for further development.

1

The Enneagram as a model

This chapter provides the answers to the following questions:

• Who developed the Enneagram?
• How is a type formed?
• Is everyone really only one type?
• Can an enneagram-type change over time?
• Are some types more likely to be men, and others women?
• Is there an equal number of each type?
• Is it always possible to see the difference between the different types?
• What is the relationship of the Enneagram to other personality typologies?
• What do the lines mean?
• Are there sub-categories within the Enneagram?
• Are other theoretical concepts contained in the Enneagram?
• To what extent has a type something to do with the neighboring type?

Who developed the Enneagram?

The Enneagram is an ancient system, the exact origins of which are unknown. You could see it as a tradition, whereby the background is not quite clear. It is comparable to the pyramids of Egypt. We can see that the construction of the pyramids is masterly, but we still don't know precisely what knowledge or science led to the visible results. It is like that with the Enneagram. The depiction of the model is known to have existed in the Middle Ages among the Sufis, a mystical tradition at the core of Islam. It is not known to what extent the model was used for psychological applications, as it is used today. Research into this is made difficult by the fact that it was only at the beginning of the 20th Century that knowledge of the Enneagram was recorded in writing, and then only to a limited extent. Before that, knowledge of the system must have been transmitted verbally. We know that the Russian philosopher and spiritual leader Gurdjieff knew about the Enneagram, although it has never been clear how he acquired his knowledge. He is the first known person to make use of the psychological information inherent in Enneagram, as we know it today. Gurdjieff posited that it was not possible for a type to recognize himself. He believed that people's defense mechanisms were too strong for them to be able to really look at their own faults and fixed patterns. He determined the individual enneagram-types of his students himself, in order to be able to guide them appropriately. Gurdjieff never committed his knowledge to writing; it was Ouspensky, one of his students, who recorded what he knew.

At the beginning of the 70s, the South American Oscar Ichazo gave training in the Enneagram to his students in Arica, Chile. Ichazo asserted that his knowledge of the Enneagram came to him independently, from a source other than Gurdjieff. One of the participants in his training was the Chilean doctor, Claudio Naranjo. Following his training in Arica, Naranjo passed on his knowledge in workshops in different locations, including California. One of Naranjo's students was the American psychologist, Helen Palmer, from whom I received my own training.

An important turning point in the development of the history of the Enneagram took place at the beginning of the 80s in the United States. Oscar Ichazo brought the first authors of Enneagram books to court for violation of copyright. Ichazo declared that the concept had been developed by him, and couldn't just be taken over by anyone. The authors were able to demonstrate that the source of the Enneagram went back much further than Ichazo, and they won the case. Since then, no one has been able to claim the concept for themselves and many experts, particularly in America, have written a great deal about it. The greatest advantage of this is that considerable knowledge of the Enneagram has become widely accessible within a relatively short time. It is meanwhile used widely, not only in companies, but also in therapy, education, pedagogy, and for personal development. A side effect of this development is that the interested reader can become confused by the many different approaches to the Enneagram with which he is confronted in the course of his exploration. It is not always easy to separate the chaff from the corn.

How is a type formed?

My premise is that the type is always there, and manifests in reaction to contact with the environment. The story of the supermarket experience illustrates the idea. In other words, everyone is predisposed towards a specific type. A musical predisposition, for instance, means that the talent for music is inherent until it is activated. Contrary to playing music, the personality and therefore the personality type are always activated as soon as the infant comes in contact with its environment. We can only see the pattern we are dealing with after it has been activated. In that respect you could compare it to children's building blocks. The child learns that the round brick only fits into the round hole, and the square one only fits into the square hole. Our personality fits into a specific hole, but we can only discover which one it is as we go through life.

Is everyone really only one type?

To answer this question properly, we need to look more closely at how the term type is understood in the Enneagram model. By model, I mean the nine-pointed star of the Enneagram. It is more correct to talk about nine different perspectives or points of view really, than to call them types. A perspective of viewpoint is neither more nor less than a position on a line. Type 1, for instance, is positioned on the line between 4 and 7. The type is therefore not in fact a point, but an angle with two lines, the center of which is where the two lines meet. In other words, Type 1 does not only possess the characteristics of Type 1. Under certain circumstances he also owns some characteristics of Types 4 and 7. Additionally, Type 1 is connected through the circle with Types 2 and 9, Type 1's neighbors, so to speak. The influence of one or two neighbors can often be observed in a type. You could see the Enneagram as a palette on which each type blends into another. Type 1 is therefore actually a combination of 5 types, connected to 4 and 7 by the lines and with 2 and 9 as the neighboring types.

Nevertheless, the perspective of each type imposes a specific order on the position given to the different viewpoints with which it is connected. In normal circumstances, Type 1 exhibits many aspects of the 1. Under stress, more of Type 4 characteristics become apparent. When Type 1 is relaxed and feels secure, he will experience more aspects of the 7. Some enneagram-type 1s will notice the influence of Type 2 characteristics; others will take on 9-type aspects. Others will feel the influence of both wings, and yet others will experience only minimal influence from their neighboring types.

It is important to realize that the enneagram-type indicates the way our attention is normally focused. However, in certain circumstances, we can see ourselves in all of the types. We all take the Type 1 perspective when standards and values are at stake. And when one of our closest friends or colleagues needs help, we all move to Type 2 to some extent or other. If we have to give a presentation to an important client about a potentially vital project, we experience the motivation that drives Type 3. We become somewhat a Type 4 when we feel moved by nature, or long for the beauty of an unspoilt environment. Studying the feasibility of a long-term project, we know what it feels like to be a 5. Having to take stock of the risks inherent in a change of course within the company, which it is our responsibility to implement, we are using the type 6 perspective. As soon as we're on holiday, having all sorts of interesting ideas about promising projects while chatting with friends over a glass of good wine, we're moving into 7 territory. When our children are threatened, all the fury and strength that is released remind others of a Type 8. And on the days when everything is going right, we're experiencing aspects of the 9 perspective.

So we know all the types, depending on the situation. The search for one type is about finding the perspective we recognize most. If the reality of daily life offers no reliable indicators, it might be useful to ask yourself which type was most applicable in the past. Our behavior usually becomes more subtly nuanced as we grow older, and this can make it difficult to uncover patterns that used to be closer to the surface.

Is it possible for an enneagram-type to change over time?

Most people experience their enneagram perspective as a constant. However, the way in which a particular perspective manifests can develop over the years. The foundation for an enneagram perspective is laid down when we are children. We are already disposed or inclined towards the development of a specific enneagram type. The enneagram perspective is often most evident between the ages of 20 and 30. The personality is then fully developed, while there is still relatively little skill or insight into the possibility of dealing with the world in alternative ways. As we grow older, all things being well, we learn two things. Firstly, we learn how to employ our enneagram perspective more effectively. We are better able to utilize our potential and control our failings. You may not know how some people begin to loosen their identification with their original perspective. If you remember the exercise at the beginning, about crossing your arms, you might say that you become more aware of alternative ways of crossing your arms. Of course, the opposite can also happen sometimes: it is possible to become more rigid as we grow older, increasingly identified with our original enneagram perspective.

You could say that one of the aims of the Enneagram is to help us become less identified with the original perspective. Now, there is a risk involved here. People might assume they have rid themselves of their original enneagram perspective. Their life experience and ability to relativise contribute to this impression. Others may see things differently, and this brings up the question of blind spots. For example, colleagues and co-workers may remark on certain patterns that they recognize in someone, yet he won't hear of it, insisting that he has put all that behind him. It might then be advisable for him to review the situation. The question remains, to what extent are we willing and able to accept the reality about ourselves? This is where the Enneagram can be an excellent tool. With its help, either alone or with others, we can learn more about the reality of others and ourselves.

Are some types more likely to be men, and others women?

This is a difficult question to answer sensibly without statistical research among a wide sample of the population. Such research has never been done. My own findings show no particular difference between men and women. Certainly, some types demonstrate more characteristics associated with either male or female behavior than others. The Type 2 perspective, for example, is more often associated with women. When we think of helping others, our first thoughts normally go to mothers, loving wives and secretaries sooner than to factory managers. However, there do appear to be differences in behavior that are stimulated by the same motivational pattern. The male Type 2 may well be more functionally oriented in the way he offers help, while the female Type 2 may focus more on emotional support. This is partly the result of differences between men and women and the socialization process. The male Type 2 in this example is not in the least less identified with the 2 perspective than the female of this type. However, it may be more difficult for others to recognize.

To take another example, Type 8 is more in accordance with the stereotype image of men. Showing strength and straightforwardness is socially accepted behavior for men. Men aren't supposed to cry, but they are allowed to be angry. It's usually exactly the reverse for women. A male 8 who gets angry is therefore often seen as a real man, while a woman risks being written off as a shrew. It may therefore be more difficult to recognize a female 8. The socialization process has already taught the woman from an early age not to express certain emotions, or to express them differently from men. Depending on the culture in which someone has grown up, you could therefore say that the motivational patterns of a type could be associated with either male or female behavior.

Does every type occur equally frequently?

Here too, there is insufficient research to be able to give a reliable answer to this question. First of all, no single environment offers an objective view. In business, there is generally over-representation of the 1, 3, 6, 7 and 8 perspectives. This is not surprising, given that these types are usually more task-oriented and extravert than the others. Types 2 and 4 are usually a little under-represented. These types are generally more focused on relationships and feelings, and business life is usually more focused on efficiency than on the development of people's emotional lives. The civil service shows greater numbers of 6's and 9's and fewer 3s, 7s and 8s. Presumably this has to do with the success of government authorities in offering consolidation and reliability. The caring professions, however, are full of 2s and 9s. Of course, it is precisely the 2 and the 9 who are born carers.

There are some national differences. In my work with international management teams, I've noticed that the culture of the country of origin often appears to overshadow the personal type. An English 3 often gives the impression of being a 5, England's national type. This seems to come from the often somewhat distant and diplomatic stance that the English adopt so well. It is only when questions of efficiency, success and image bring out strong confirmation of a Type 3 profile, that the distant stance can be seen as the influence of the culture of origin, and we discover that we're dealing with a type 3, not a 5. You might often take an American 5 or 9 for a 3, but there is a good chance that it is the influence of the cultural type that is hiding his true motivation.

Is it always possible to see the difference between the different types?

It can be difficult. It is possible to have a look-alike situation, where two types resemble each other. For example, it is not always easy to distinguish a 9 from a 2. Both types are relationship-oriented and likely to help others. In this case it is important to investigate the possible differences between the types. These differences can't always be discovered in their behavior, which is after all where the resemblance can be observed. What is needed is more information about their driving forces, the underlying motivation that leads to the apparently similar behavior. The Enneagram shows that it is indeed possible for identical behavior to be founded on different incentives. His longing for harmony therefore quite likely motivates the relationship orientation of Type 9. Type 2 is more inclined to focus on others because of his need to help them and for the possible approval this could bring him. However, Type 9 may also resemble Type 5 under certain circumstances. Both types are generally more introvert than extravert. Here too, it is important to examine where the differences lie. Type 5 is usually introverted in an effort to protect his own space, while the 9 is more likely to take the attitude that he has nothing to say.

Types 6 and 8 can also look quite similar to each other in their ability to be direct and even confrontational. But Type 6 employs confrontation out of a necessity for clarity and safety. For him, confrontation may well be experienced as a necessary evil. Type 8 however, often finds confrontation the most interesting way to find out more about others and their opinions. Here too, the behavior may look identical, but the reasons for it are quite different.

All of the types can be explored in this way to see their similarities and differences. In my experience, it is almost always possible to differentiate the different types through investigation of their underlying motivation, rather than by their behavior.

How does the Enneagram compare with other personality typologies?

There are many useful models and systems based on personality typologies. The methods most often used in management training are the Myers Briggs Type Indicator (MBTI), the Life Style Inventory (LSI), Life Orientations (LIFO), Belbin's Team Roles, Quinn's Management Styles, and PAPI and Graves' color coding system. All of these methods are useful in that they help to differentiate patterns of behavior, motivation and/or the preferred roles of people in organizations. They all have the potential of benefiting us through a better understanding of others and ourselves.

The Enneagram differs from most other methods by reason of its primary emphasis on motivation rather than on behavior. As is apparent with the look-alikes, it is possible to have totally different incentives for identical behavior. If we want to influence ourselves or other people, we need to understand the underlying motivation, because this is the source of the behavior. The Enneagram also shows how one type may exhibit very different types of behavior. If we didn't know what the basic need was, this would make it difficult to place the behavior.

Knowledge of motivation allows us to understand how apparently contradictory behavior may result from one and the same source.

One consequence of the fact that the Enneagram mainly looks for motivational patterns is, that it often takes longer to determine a type than with more behavior-oriented methods. When an organization establishes better self-awareness as one of its goals, this is in itself a very interesting event. In my experience, the process of determining one's own type can be almost as beneficial as knowing what that type is.

Another difference between the Enneagram and most other methods is that no one person or authority holds the copyright for the Enneagram model. (See: Who developed the Enneagram?). For this reason, a great deal of information about the Enneagram is freely accessible. Part 3 of this book suggests a number of books in which various experts describe their knowledge of the Enneagram and its possible applications.

What do the lines mean?

The lines between types indicate what happens under stress or when we are relaxed. In stressful situations, we move in the direction of the arrows, and against them when relaxed or secure. But the story doesn't end there. What the Enneagram highlights is how our attention is oriented in a different way under varying circumstances. This probably sounds logical to most people. The interesting point here is that the Enneagram clearly shows how reactions to stress or relaxed situations are very different depending on the type concerned. Type 1 behavior is therefore normal for a 1, but is only exhibited by a 7 in stressful situations. And from the perspective of a 4, the position of 1 is associated with relaxation.

The Enneagram is not a static model. It is a systematic process that encourages awareness and the personal development that develops from it. Originally, the assumption was that there was a particular advantage in learning what happened in stress situations. In order to know what you needed to learn, you only had to follow your own type in the direction of the arrow. A Type 7 would therefore have most to learn in the Type 1 position. In practice however, practically everyone can gain just as much insight by moving to a perspective in which we feel relaxed. In this sense, the direction of the arrow has only relative value for the learning or development process.

• Disintegration and integration

There are different interpretations of the connecting lines. Enneagram expert Riso refers to a process of disintegration or integration. For example, when the 6 takes on aspects of the 3 perspective, they are usually the negative characteristics of that type. This is something that it is therefore preferable to avoid, and when it happens it is a sign of disintegration. In Riso's view, the 6's move towards the 9 would be the sign of an integrated personality. In this case, it is the positive characteristics of the 9 that are assumed. In other words, the disintegration position indicates the weaknesses of the type, while the integrated position describes the type's potential for improvement.

• Stress and security

Palmer refers to stress and security responses in her discussion of the lines. Our stress response is to move in the direction of the arrow, and our security response is to move against the arrow, relaxing into the type behind our own. Her view is that we take on both the positive and the negative characteristics of the respective type in situations of stress or security. Type 1 when relaxed would therefore not only take on the playful and positive aspects of the 7, but may also encounter the irresponsible and excessive pleasure-seeking tendencies of this type. And in stress situations, the 1 may have to contend with the imbalance of the 4, but could also experience this type's heightened sensitivity.

• Original qualities

A.H. Almaas, another expert in the area of the Enneagram, gives yet another view of the lines. His approach does not associate the point of relaxation in the first instance with potential security. The qualities belonging to the type towards which we move in relaxed situations are seen as qualities belonging to the state of being experienced prior to identification with the personality. In terms of the metaphor used in connection with little Ben, they are the qualities embodied by the child before the fortress was constructed. The examples of 'pure love' and 'pure trust' were named in that connection, but there are of course many other qualities. In this approach, one or more of these qualities belong to each type. The line of relaxation therefore shows what the original qualities were, before becoming obscured beneath the construction. In the terminology of Almaas, this is the soul child, the original soul of the child. One of the purposes of personal development is to regain contact with the soul child we have always been, but have lost our connection to. The point of relaxation therefore offers insight into this, allowing us to catch a glimpse of what we lost.

To summarize, it could be said that knowledge of the stress point helps us to recognize symptoms of stress in others and ourselves. The Enneagram demonstrates that stress can be experienced in different ways by different types, and that in this connection, our own mechanisms are not the measure of how things are for everyone.

Knowledge of the point of relaxation, among other things, is a way of clarifying how we could develop further. Whether through the insight that it is good to feel secure (Palmer), through the insight that it is admirable to develop our potential and thereby become integrated (Riso), or because our potential lies hidden in the discovery of what we have currently lost contact with, but essentially still are (Almaas), all of these approaches provide guidance in directing our own development and that of others.

Are there sub-categories within the Enneagram?

The nine Enneagram types can be sub-divided into three categories of three types.

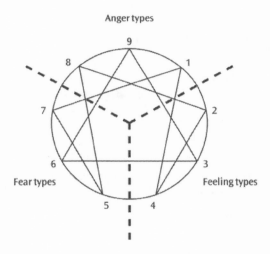

Types 2, 3 and 4 are Feeling types. Types 5, 6 and 7 are known as Fear types. Types 8, 9 and 1 belong to the category known as the Anger types. The following will clarify what is meant by these categories.

• Feeling types 2, 3 and 4

It is not because they are the only types to have feelings that Types 2, 3 and 4 are called the Feeling types. Every individual, and therefore every type, has feelings. With these types however, it is their feelings or distortions of them that are most likely to influence the way they orient their attention.

Type 2 distorts his feelings and sensitivity by not paying attention to how he feels, focusing instead on the feelings of others in order to be able to provide what they need. The ability to feel is primarily oriented towards sensing what someone else needs. For Type 2, the growth edge is therefore learning to use his sensitivity to become more aware of his own feelings, as well as those of other people.

Type 3 either ignores his feelings if it looks as if they might interfere with efficiency, or uses his feeling ability primarily to achieve success. Ask a 3 to what he attributes his successes and he is likely to explain that they were not the result of a long intellectual process, but that he acted on his feelings. He has a gut feel for whether or not a project will be a success. It is thanks to his sensitivity that the 3 is able to make fast decisions with successful results. Should the 3 notice personal feelings that could threaten the efficient achievement of his goal, he will know how to minimize them, or at least post pone them until his work is finished. The lesson for Type 3 is to learn how to allow his feelings to contribute more empathy and sensitivity to his way of dealing with himself and others at work and in private life, as well as in the interests of achieving success in his career.

Type 4 also has a highly developed emotional life, but assigns so much importance to it that he is overwhelmed. Because emotions change like the weather, this is how the 4 experiences reality. Life becomes an endless cycle of highs and lows, peaks and troughs. The insight offered to Type 4 is that while feelings enrich life, they are not all there is to it.

Types 2, 3 and 4 are also known as the heart types, because the heart is the part of the body where feelings of love and affection, sadness and hurt are most strongly experienced.

• Fear Types 5, 6 and 7

Here too, Types 5, 6 and 7 are of course not the only types to experience fear. Everyone can experience fear, and so all of the types may be subject to fear at times. Fear doesn't belong to these three types alone, but it is the feeling of fear or a distortion of it that strongly influences the way in which they focus their attention.

Because of the impact that fear has on thinking, it manifests primarily in how these types think. For Type 5, fear is a stimulus to thinking of ways to protect his feelings from the outside world. Thinking creates a division between the inside and the outside world, caused by fear that the outside world would otherwise trample on the vulnerable feelings inside. The challenge for the 5 is not to allow fear to cause his suffering, and to investigate the emotional barriers that he erects between himself and the outside world.

Fear affects the thinking of Type 6 through doubt. The 6 not only doubts himself, but projects doubt onto others by thinking that they are not to be trusted, or in the other extreme, believing the other to be an authority, someone who knows better. It is important for the 6 to verify whether his fear is based on fact, or is merely an illusion created by his thoughts.

Type 7 is also driven by fear, particularly the fear of having to confront unpleasantness. Thinking converts the fear into wonderful ideas and plans, so that a possibly threatening confrontation with reality can be avoided. The growth edge for Type 7s is to learn to face their fearful emotions, often experienced in anticipation of humdrum routine and boredom.

Types 5, 6 and 7 are also known as the head types, because the fear felt by these types is primarily influenced by their thinking.

• Anger types 8, 9 and 1

Again, the 8, 9 and 1 known as the Anger Types are not the sole possessors of feelings of anger, but are influenced by this emotion or its distortion in the way they view the world.

Type 8 is the most likely of these three to come in contact with the feeling of anger. Type 8 has no difficulty in expressing his emotions, but must learn to adapt them to his environment. The process involves learning to intervene before the emotion of anger is converted to impulsive outbursts, with all of consequences this usually entails.

Anger is also an important source of energy for Type 9, but the 9 suppresses his anger because it is seen as a threat to the harmony he so values. As a result, the 9 stores up his anger. The 9 has the memory of an elephant, and will remember his anger for so long that very little may finally goad him into showing it. His anger may also find expression indirectly by not reacting, inaction, or otherwise going into silent opposition. The Type 9 can learn to become more aware of his own anger and express his feelings of discontentment more straightforwardly.

Anger also has considerable influence on the way in which the 1 orients his attention. The 1's dilemma is how to behave as he feels he ought to. A direct expression of anger does not usually conform to this image. But because anger is a strong emotion, it has to find some form of expression. The method often chosen by a 1 is humiliation. Behind an explanation of how something should or should not be done, there is often a great deal of hidden anger that the world doesn't understand how things ought to be. Those around a 1 are often more aware of his anger than he himself. The task for a Type 1 is to learn to be more aware of the anger he feels.

I work with this sub-categorization of the types only to a limited extent in my own workshops. Terminology that divide the types into feeling, anger and fear groups require very careful explanation to avoid falling into undifferentiated stereotyping which does not do full justice to the truth. All the same, for those interested in the emotions underlying the ennea-gram-types, this is interesting material. Several of the books mentioned in the bibliography go more deeply into this approach.

Are other theoretical concepts contained in the Enneagram?

Each type can be included in three subtypes. The subtypes refer to methods of self-preservation, ways in which we participate in groups and how we relate to a special friend. There are 27 subtypes in all.

The division into subtypes is based on three psychological stages of development. During these stages, the foundations are laid for the development of the relevant subtype. As explained earlier, formation of a type begins in the first years of our life. Our early development can be divided into three phases. The first phase occurs in the first years of life and mostly has to do with survival. So long as we are given enough to eat and drink in a caring manner, we survive. As children, we begin to notice after a few years that it is not only important to have enough to eat and drink in order to survive, but that it is also important to be able to get along with those closest to us. This process is clearly visible with infants when they begin to enjoy playing with other children, for exam-ple, rather than being contented to amuse themselves. This is the second phase. The third phase follows when we notice that it is not enough just to be able to get on with all kinds of other children; we want a special friend with whom to form a bond. Children then begin to talk about 'my boyfriend' or 'my girlfriend', to emphasize the special relationship. In later years the need for a special person in our lives naturally acquires a different meaning, generally connected with a sexual relationship.

To be able to function effectively, the personality needs strategies for survival, as in phase 1, in order to handle relationships with groups, as in phase 2, and to be able to engage in an intimate relation-ship, as in phase 3. Although these mechanisms appear during a specific phase of childhood, they remain applicable for the duration of our lives, because of the direct link made to their effectiveness.

The Enneagram shows that a difference can be made between strategies used by each type for survival, group relationships and one-on-one relationships. These strategies are also referred to as sub-types. Each type has its own way of handling these three processes successfully and has developed its own strategies to do so. Each type therefore disposes over all three strategies or subtypes. There are different opinions about the way in which these manifest among different Enneagram experts. Some say we all have one favorite subtype. Others say that we use all three, independently of the circumstances or our age group.

To what extent is a type related to its neighboring type?

Students of the Enneagram will notice that the types are not only connected to other types at their stress and relaxation points, but also bear a relationship to the neighboring types through their position on the circle. These neighboring points are the 'wings' of a type. Type 3 therefore has a 2 wing and a 4 wing. The Enneagram might be compared to a palette of colors in which the colors complement and to some extent blend into each other. It is often so that someone who has determined his own type notices that he also recognizes the influence of one of the neighboring types. This neighboring type gives a certain flavor to the main type. A Type 7 with a 6 wing is often somewhat more cautious or fearful than the 7 without a 6 wing. The 7 with an 8 wing may be more direct and confrontational than the same type without an 8 wing. Some Enneagram experts believe that a wing always influences the type. Others assume this to be a possibility, but not a necessity. Yet others speak of the influence of one wing only, while again others base their view on the possibility of two wings.

In my own experience, the influence of a neighboring type is clearly apparent in certain cases. The degree of this influence varies. Some people experience a strong influence from the wing, while others notice only limited effects. I have seen less evidence of the presence of two wings. I would add that I prefer to be somewhat reticent about putting an emphasis on the wings in my workshops. When someone has determined their own type, it can be interesting to investigate the extent to which there may be an influence from one of the neighboring types. If there is, it can be the source of additional, complementary insight. The usefulness of the concept of the wings to help determine a type is limited. Someone who recognizes themselves in the 1, the 2 and the 6 may start to think he could be either a 1 or a 2, because they adjoin each other. However, this approach is more likely to confuse that clarify. The wing is probably most usefully seen as interesting supplementary information that allows a more differentiated light to be thrown on the type, after it has been determined.

2

The Enneagram in Business

This chapter provides the answers to the following questions:

• Are certain Enneagram types more likely to be found in some functions than in others?

• To what extent can the Enneagram be used for the purposes of recruitment and selection?

• How helpful is the Enneagram in the creation of management or project teams?

• How can management or project teams make use of the Enneagram?

• In practice, do certain situations tend to occur more frequently than others?

• What is the central issue for managers and teams: learning to accept ourselves and others, or using the Enneagram to bring about change?

• How can the Enneagram be helpful in project management?

• Do certain types of organization attract certain Enneagram type employees?

• What are the risks associated with use of the Enneagram in companies?

• Does use of the Enneagram cause stereotyping?

• How does the Enneagram type of an organization develop?

• To what extent can the Enneagram typology of an organization be changed?

• Are there any interesting commercial applications for the Enneagram?

Are certain Enneagram types more likely to be found in some functions than in others?

Yes, that has been my experience. But we have to be careful about the conclusions to be drawn from this. I will give you a few examples. Types 1 and 6 are usually well represented among accountants and controllers. This is hardly surprising. These professions require a combination of carefulness and a critical attitude. That does not mean that all accountants of Type 1 or 6 are careful and critical by definition. Nor does it mean that an enneagram-type 4 accountant is not careful or critical, and therefore cannot be a good accountant. Knowledge of the type offers information about our primary focus, the rough diamond of our personality, as it were, before we learned from experience how to adapt it to suit our environment. It does not provide information about all that we have learned in the course of our lives. This question requires closer observation in each individual case.

It is indeed so that the Enneagram gives insight into the potential qualities of a type. In order to allow optimal development within a particular function or career, it is important to find an environment where these qualities are appreciated. From this point of view, different enneagram-types naturally feel attracted to some functions rather than others.

To what extent can the Enneagram be used for the purposes of recruitment and selection?

It can be helpful in certain circumstances. To begin with, it is important to remember that the Enneagram is not a normative method. The enneagram-type does not tell us anything about the degree to which someone may demonstrate effective or counter-productive behavior, it shows the framework within which certain behavior may occur. But the fulfillment of a function requires insight into the effectiveness of someone's behavior, and this is something the Enneagram cannot show. The following bell-curve illustrates the point.

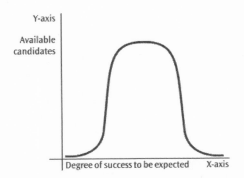

The y-axis gives information about the number of available candidates. The x-axis shows the degree of success to be expected in a function. In the selection process, you will naturally be interested in the candidates situated at the extreme right of the graph. This candidate promises the highest success factor in the job. To a certain extent, it won't matter very much what type this person is. If the selection is made primarily according to type, it could be that a person matches the expected type, but is situated at the left side of the bell-curve; precisely what you don't want.

If the selection process is intended to find candidates to be groomed for a career, rather than for a specific position, then the learning ability of the candidate will be of primary importance. The Enneagram offers no information here either. However, if the enneagram-type is known, it could be used to differentiate a candidate's learning ability. For example, it would be useful to know how he has dealt with his qualities and weaknesses until now, and what he has learned from his experience. It would be relevant to ask a type 9, for instance, what he has learned about decision-making, how he handles conflict and what he knows about time management. How the candidate answers questions provides information about his self-awareness and ability to learn.

To use this approach, it is of course of the utmost importance that the recruiter or person leading the selection process is sure of his facts concerning the candidate's enneagram-type.

How helpful is the Enneagram in the creation of management or project teams?

The points considered in connection with recruitment and selection are also applicable to the creation of teams. The key to the creation of effective teams is the ability and willingness of the manager to take his own and others' behavior patterns into consideration. The types that team members are is not the issue. Here too, each person concerned must be considered individually.

It is true, of course, that every team has inherent opportunities and pitfalls. Some time ago, I coached an 8-man management team of whom four represented the type 8 perspective, three found the 3 viewpoint most applicable to themselves, and the chairman was obviously a 5. Although the 5 leader had a high degree of insight into himself and others, it was clear that good management of his team would present a considerable challenge.

I also knew a team where all nine types were represented. The enneagram-types were not specifically considered in the creation of the team, although great value was attached to achieving complementarity. Attention was not only given to differences in function, but also to differences in personality. Provided that the differences are taken into consideration, such a wide variety of types can increase the quality of teamwork enormously.

When the Enneagram is used to help create teams, advice concerning variations of the types is never something to be followed blindly; the effectiveness of the individuals concerned plays an important role. However, the enneagram-type information can provide additional information about which roles are more likely to suit one person rather than another. For instance, I have seldom seen a Type 8 function well in teams where he was responsible for the consolidation of activities or developments. Type 8 does much better in a situation where his entre-preneurship and responsibility is more in demand. A type 5 who is made responsible for commercial success in the short term is likely to face a considerable challenge. On the other hand, the type 5 will proba-bly be able to give good account of himself in the role of knowledge gatherer/developer.

As already mentioned, making automatic links between type and function is rash. In practice, I have seen a Type 5 manager choose a commercial function that did not suit his personality at all. He was aware of this, and his choice was a deliberate one in order to acquire commercial skills. It was also clear to him that this was not his vocation, and he did not intend to dedicate more than two years to the experi-ence. His employer agreed that this would be an interesting learning experience for him within the framework of management develop-ment, and supported his move, in spite of the fact that better candidates were available for the job. The manager returned to a more strategic function after two years, and had undoubtedly acquired very valuable business experience meanwhile.

How can management or project teams make use of the Enneagram?

Management and project teams can use the Enneagram as a tool to improve co-operation both within and outside the team. When the Enneagram is delivered in the form of team training, it involves different steps. Firstly, interviews are used to make an inventory of the opportunities and pitfalls for the team as a whole and for its individual members. Then typing interviews are held. The goal of a typing interview is to determine each person's enneagram-type as precisely as possible. Then the team workshop begins. During the workshop, all enneagram-types are discussed in depth. Those team members whose type is under discussion are asked to come forward and answer a number of questions about their type. This allows other team members to get a better picture of the thoughts, feelings and behavior of their colleagues. Experience shows that team members understand each other relatively easily and take things less personally. "Now I understand why you always..." is a frequent comment of colleagues after they have heard one of their number speak about his type.

The next step is to ask team members to describe situations between themselves and one or more others outside the team, where they wish to improve communication. This could have to do with a boss, a co-worker or a customer. The team members are asked to consider what the possible enneagram-type of the person in question might be. Sometimes this is quite easy. At other times the type remains an assumption, or there appears to be clear indications of two or even three types. When the actual situations have been formulated, they are demonstrated with the help of an actor. The actor, fully versed in the Enneagram, is given all the background information so that he can enact the behavior of the customer, co-worker or boss in the situation described. The team member who proposed the situation is now asked to enter into a dialogue with the actor, just as he would in real life. In spite of being an artificially created situation, recognition of the opponent and the way in which the dialogue proceeds is usually extraordinarily clear. The ensuing discussion brings to light how interaction between certain enneagram-types in specific situations usually occurs, and how it could be improved.

In addition to this work, an analysis of the composition of the team is carried out. When the enneagram-type becomes clear, its relevant qualities and failings can be looked at in terms of the function fulfilled by each person. The potential of relationships between different types within the team can also be examined. If all team members are clear about their own type, an analysis can be made of the potential strong and weak points of the team, their opportunities and threats. It is always important to bear in mind that the type by no means expresses anything about the effectiveness of an individual. Neither is any one type better than any other. Finally, an analysis may be made of the possible enneagram-type of the organizational culture, and its implications for the team.

Are some situations more likely to occur than others?

Many practical situations concern relationships with the boss. Those concerning colleagues, clients or co-workers actually only arise where there is conflict. This used to surprise me, because I thought that the most important concern of a leader was his interactions with his staff. Experience proves otherwise. I think there are two explanations for this. The first has to do with the dynamics of organizations. The second explanation is of a more psychological nature.

In most organizations, a career path is determined to a much greater extent by the judgment of the boss than that of co-workers. It is therefore more important that our boss is satisfied with us, than that our co-workers, colleagues or clients are. Of course, there is a connection. But in most organizations, we can achieve a great deal when we are able to explain to the boss why things are going as they are, or we find some other way of compensating for our deficiencies. From this point of view, it is more efficient to invest in our relationship with our superiors than with anyone else.

The second explanation is more psychological in nature. Organizations are hierarchical institutions. Generally speaking, there is an accepted form of mild dictatorship. Authoritarian directives, which we would consider unacceptable in the context of national laws, are seen as a necessary evil within the company. This acceptance of authority is something we recognize from our childhood. Up to a certain age, our parents were our bosses, and quite rightly. Psychologically, we always associate present situations with similar situations in the past. The role our boss plays in terms of a position of power can best be compared with the role our father or mother played when we were small. Because the association is so strong, our relationship with the boss often triggers the same feelings as those we had as children. Male leaders at work will usually have images of the father projected onto them, while female bosses are burdened with projections of mother. And because the relationship with our parents is one of the most influential in most of our lives, the reaction to a boss is often pervaded with old images and feelings concerning parental figures. We are also often more liable to consider ourselves as the underdog in relation to our bosses, and more in control of others, such as co-workers. This difference in power also plays an important role in the situation with the boss.

What is the central issue: Learning to accept ourselves and others, or using the Enneagram to bring about change?

It has as much to do with acceptance as with change. The question therefore becomes, when to apply one and when the other? Every manager knows the dilemma: Should I accept that this person is the way he is and focus on providing optimal support, or should I set limits and confront him with my expectations? This is a theme that pops up in every coaching role: trainers, coaches and consultants are confronted with the same dilemma in their own work. I think myself that change is difficult if acceptance of the current reality has not first been achieved. This doesn't mean that we have to applaud this approach, but it is important to understand why someone is doing what he is doing, or is the way he is. After all, it isn't very encouraging to show the truth about ourselves or a situation if we are not more or less sure that it won't be used against us.

My experience is that when there is true understanding of the feelings, thoughts and behavior of others, a natural movement towards change can occur. This mechanism is made apparent in Enneagram workshops by initially asking participants to talk exclusively about their own thoughts and feelings. There is no emphasis on how anyone could or should change. Nevertheless, it often appears that the participants do in fact experience change after this exercise. Apparently something changes in ourselves when we air our thoughts. This is a familiar phenomenon, quite apart from the Enneagram. It happens when we have an opportunity to talk over important thoughts and feelings with a good friend or colleague. Even without the other person saying or doing anything, apart from listening attentively, we might feel that bringing something out into the open has allowed it to fall into place.

When similar processes occur in team situations, it is useful to examine mutual expectations concerning the challenges facing the team on the basis of better knowledge of each other, and possibly renewed attitudes of mutual respect and acceptance. It helps to make agreements about this that can be evaluated and adjusted if necessary.

How can the Enneagram help with project management?

The success of projects usually appears to be less dependent on the methodology of the project, than on the way in which people do or do not co-operate with others. Project managers often notice how other colleagues with the same degree of know-how and in much the same circumstances, nevertheless complete their projects more efficiently, or less well than themselves. The human factor, the ability to deal with other people, is what makes the difference.

The Enneagram can help to become more aware of the human factor in project management, and indicates how to give better leadership. If a project manager has some insight into his own enneagram-type, it is relatively easy to identify his strengths and weaknesses in management. The next step is to figure out how to make optimal use of this knowledge. A great deal of experience has been acquired in project management workshops concerning the application of the Enneagram as a method of improving the human factor in project management. We give considerable attention to the project manager achieving awareness of his own typology. Current projects are then used to formulate situations requiring the attention of project managers. They may have to do with situations with customers or co-workers on the project. Based on the available facts, a possible enneagram-profile of all those concerned with the project is determined. The situation is then portrayed with the help of a professional actor. This allows the project manager to become more aware of himself and his influence on the direct environment. The ultimate goal is that the project manager integrates this knowledge into his project management style.

Do certain types of organization attract certain enneagram-type employees?

That is the impression I have. For several years, I trained managers from a successful multinational organization in recruitment interviewing. The company in question had a pronounced enneagram-type 6 profile: loyalty, analytic ability, reliability and friendliness were its core qualities. The tendency was to attract staff who at least fit this profile. Of course there is absolutely nothing amiss with the Type 6 profile, but there was a risk of under-representing certain qualities, like creativity or entrepreneurship. With a certain amount of self-mockery, this 'cloning' tendency was ridiculed in one of the internal company newsletters. A cartoon showed two identical men sitting opposite each other at a desk. The man behind the desk was saying, "You're exactly the man we're looking for." The cartoon was of course intended to initiate discussion about the way in which recruitment and selection was carried out within the organization. There was a need to bring about less cloning and more variety among the managerial ranks.

The Enneagram can help to bring such tendencies to light. But even when a conscious effort is made to find staff with a different profile, in practice the company will still attract more people of their own organizational type than other organizations. It is my impression that it is not easy to change an organization by employing people with a totally different profile. Patience and care are recommended here. You may find some of a new generation leaving the company within a few years, in the belief that they will be happier somewhere else.

Of course, it is not all necessary for employees to have the same enneagram profile as the company, but it is important for them to be able to get along with it. Some time ago, a senior manager from a large international company requested a few sessions with me. He had been extremely successful in his previous job, but his new employer didn't appear to have the same appreciation for his approach. After some study, it turned out that he recognized himself most in the enneagram 3 perspective. His previous company was a Type 3 organization, where efficiency, internal competitiveness and individual excellence were written large. His new company appeared to be a 9 organization. Here, the qualities most likely to achieve results were deliberation and harmony. As a Type 3 in a 3 company, the manager was very successful: his competitive behavior was appreciated, his ambitions were given free range and no barriers were put in the way of his goal-oriented and efficient method of working. But the same behavior caused all sorts of problems in the new, type 9 organization. His competitiveness was interpreted as lack of solidarity with his colleagues, his ambitions were considered too pretentious and a high degree of efficiency was frequently considered unachievable by the existing consensus culture. The prohibitive reaction of his environment made him unsure of himself and reinforced his own 3 patterns. He started to work harder and became even more ambitious, causing an unavoidable spiral of reaction.

In fact, the manager and the company spoke two different languages, without being able to understand each other. As soon as this pattern became apparent, the manager was better able to understand the language of the organization and to adapt his own behavior accordingly. It became clear to him that he could learn a lot from working for a while in an organization that was so differently oriented. On the other hand, this example shows how difficult it is to understand personalities who apparently do not fit in with their company culture.

Some years ago, in order to clarify the dynamics between the individual and the organizational culture, we carried out an analysis of the profile of the most successful managers in an international company, within the framework of a management development program for the company. They appeared to operate broadly from the perspective of the enneagram-type 3. We examined what this would mean for an employee of a different enneagram-type whose ambition it was to reach the top echelons of the company. From the point of view of management development, we were able to determine the relative flexibility of the organization in creating an optimal context for future top managers. The results offered several pointers for focused coaching which could be offered to managers who apparently did not match the success-profile of a top manager, but actually had the right potential.

What are the risks of using the Enneagram in companies?

The risks are stereotyping and stigmatization. The Enneagram is intended to provide a tool to help us understand ourselves and others better. This understanding comes about because of taking the trouble to examine ourselves and listen carefully to others about how they see their own type. I have had the experience that one team began to assign type numbers to their colleagues outside the team after an Enneagram workshop, although these colleagues had not participated in the workshop themselves. Quite apart from the question of whether their conclusions were correct, the colleagues in question were naturally grossly short-changed. This can happen quite easily on a smaller scale, for example by categorizing colleagues immediately according to type behavior: "He's a type 8, so I'll never get him to listen to me…" or "As a 6, he will probably never agree to this…" and the like. I've seen the leader of a management team putting the enneagram-type number on the office-doors of all of the managers beside their names after a workshop. Although it was meant well and intended to remind everyone of their own and others' types for the purposes of improving communication, some of the team felt humiliated and shown up within the company.

Knowledge is power, and that is no less true of knowledge of men. Knowledge of the Enneagram can be a helpful tool in bringing about more respect and care for human relationships in organizations, but it can also be used to hurt people. When the system is implemented with good intentions, the latter will rarely occur.

Does use of the Enneagram cause stereotyping?

Stereotyping always occurs to some extent. People have their preferences. Groups and individuals continually tend to classify and attach labels. We use gender, origin, religion, sexual preference, education, salary scales and income to categorize people. Certain classifications acquire a positive label within some groups, while a different social context may give the same label a negative slant. The same is true of personality characteristics. Even without knowledge of the Enneagram, we tend to classify people, as introverts and extraverts, for example. Certain groups will have more affinity with introverts, while others assign more value to extraverts.

The positive or negative associations that we have with different character traits often have little to do with the person in question. They are primarily based on our earlier experiences of people with similar traits. These experiences may have been positive, negative or neutral. Later, we project the images created by our experiences onto the person we assume to have the same characteristics. Other people are frequently little more than a projection screen, onto which we project our own pictures. Unless we look more closely, our mind assumes that our own images—which are the thoughts and feelings the other person triggers in us—are in fact applicable to that person. The projection mechanism is always at work in human relations, but it becomes more clearly visible when we work with the Enneagram. Everyone begins to notice positive or negative associations with different types. The associations are often based on earlier experiences with people who embodied that specific type. Such projections are one of the most important barriers to good communication in general and especially within organizations. The

Enneagram shows that the nature of the projections is reasonably predictable. It is relatively easy to make a list of characteristics which others
do or don't like about a type. It is also possible to indicate the projections that are likely to be made by each type.

To counteract the negative effects of projection as much as possible,
this is how the issue is handled in workshops. Before a panel member is
asked to give information about his type, all participants do an exercise
in which they investigate what associations they have with the relevant
type and what people they know or have known who remind them of it.
The participants exchange information with each other about these
experiences and associations. You could call it a gossip session. This
activates images that exist in any case, but may have been forgotten. The
different images are then recorded. Sometimes they are more positively
nuanced, sometimes negatively. The participants then do an exercise in
which they are asked to release these images and to listen to the panel as
openly as possible. Because of the process of bringing the various
images to consciousness, there is less chance of them immediately being
projected onto their colleague on the panel. The better colleagues have
known each other before the workshop, the stronger the projections
they have already made in association with the relevant person, and the
more difficult it is to let go of them again.

How does the Enneagram type of an organization develop?

Little investigation has been done into the development of organizational types. I can only speak from my own experience. To begin with,
the same applies for the organizational type as for the individual: this is
a modeled assumption about the reality and as such, can never fully
describe reality. The type is a map that is used to learn more about the
reality. While it has a functional application, it is not reality itself. That
is much more differentiated and colorful.

One single type seldom applies exclusively within an organization. Taking one organization as an example, Shell has a predominantly 6 company culture. The characteristics of Type 6 that can be found within Shell concern the traditional, worldwide loyalty of their employees, rewarded—at least until recently—with lifetime employment. Type 6 elements are also apparent in the ability to plan ahead; it is not for nothing that the expression scenario planning originated in a company like Shell. Decision-making is based on carefully substantiated studies, and the execution of tasks and projects is regulated with clear procedures. The Type 6 ability to build a strong internal network is also apparent. Until recently, the latter was expressed in an attitude towards the outside world that saw it as a potential threat requiring management, rather than a possible partner for co-operation in solving problems. A number of these characteristics are the logical result of being a company involved in petrochemical activities, where continuity combined with long-term industrial processes play an important role.

The cultural aspects mentioned here can be found all over the world within Shell. But if you look at Shell's sales organizations, you will find more signs of a 3 culture, oriented towards fast decisions and smooth adaptation to the consumer's needs. And Shell's research centers have always had a strong 5 culture—unsurprisingly really, given research centers oriented towards the development of in-depth knowledge in the interests of future technologies. The refineries are more of a mixture of 6 and 8 cultures, which is also understandable in the light of their activities. Departments and divisions within an organization can therefore have a different dominant typology than the organization as a whole. Since strategic decision-making primarily occurs at the top of an organization, this is where the dominant overall typology is generally more visible.

But this still does not answer the question about how an organiza-tional typology comes into being. I see various causal factors. Family-run and relatively entrepreneurial organizations tend to be strongly influenced by the typology of their founders; thus their typology influ-ences the development of the organizational type. Entrepreneurs often appear to be 8s, undoubtedly because the 8 doesn't like to be bossed around and probably comes to the conclusion that it is therefore better to be his own boss. A number of family-run companies have a clearly recognizable 8 culture. This is visible in the relative absence of formal rules, and a concentration of power around a few people within the organization. This set-up frequently leads to big problems when it comes to questions of succession. The Type 8 entrepreneur is not always aware that he is holding so much power and excluding subordinates with an equal amount of power, but differing points of view from his own. This attitude may cause managers to leave or avoid joining such an organization in the first place, making it difficult to find suitable suc-cessors within the organization. An inelegant, but dramatic example of a Type 8 organization is the Mafia. The power of the Mafia has always resided in the protective attitude of the organization towards its mem-bers. The downside is its all-or-nothing approach.

In the case of multinationals, the land of origin of the company often has an influence on its enneagram typology. It is no mere coincidence that American organizations like McKinsey, Anderson Consulting, Nike, McDonalds and PriceWaterhouseCoopers have a distinctly 3 cul-ture. The elements of the 3 that are to be found in such organizations are the ability to create a successful image, an attitude that overtime is normal, a culture in which competition is encouraged, and winners are openly rewarded. Giving time and attention to deliberation and long-term investments is often more difficult for this type of organization.

A 4 country like Italy produces more 4-type companies like Olivetti and members of the Fiat organization. The unequalled precision and top quality of the Swiss watchmaker Rolex originates in the Type 1 Swiss culture. The Netherlands as a 9 produces its Type 9 organizations, of which the Dutch Railway is just one interesting example. Elements of the 9 that can be found in several leading Dutch companies have to do with a culture of consensus. The positive side of this is that many people contribute to the decisions that are made. The drawback is the length of time it takes to arrive at a decision, partly because of the 9's relative lack of ability to express a straightforward opinion. The lengthy decision-making process often astounds many non-Dutch managers assigned to a posting in The Netherlands, where consensus is required at every level of the organization. Other Type 9 characteristics are the pleasant social climate, employee's willingness to listen to what everyone has to say, a high degree of tolerance and the space given to personal development. Considering the Dutch culture, these characteristics are not altogether surprising.

The primary process of an organization also has a strong influence on its Enneagram typology. The caring professions probably have a strong 2 culture everywhere in the world. Many information and communication technology industries, such as many Silicone Valley companies, possess a dominant 7 culture. The power of these organizations lies in their ability to generate a large number of ideas and concepts at high speed, and quickly create enthusiasm for them in the marketplace. Many 5 elements are often to be seen within universities and research institutes. Accountancy and other professional organizations may emphasize characteristics of the Type 1. A Type 6 culture may dominate in organizations calling for a responsible attitude and successful method of handling of future risk prognoses. Many financial institutes have a Type 6 culture, although a company like Shell is also a good example here. It is also to be found in some government bodies and in the police force.

To what extent can the Enneagram typology of an organization be altered?

Just as with the individual typology, changing the type is not really the issue. It is more interesting to consider how to develop the qualities belonging to a type, and how to avoid its weaknesses. It is also important to remember the points of stress and relaxation. Reorganization often pushes companies towards their stress position. The 7 organization moves towards 1, and can become inflexible. The 9 organization moves towards 6 under stress, and becomes suspicious and skeptical. The 6 takes on more aspects of the 3, and gets itself into deep water because of overwork. The growth area for organizations often lies at the point of relaxation. It is interesting for the 6 organization to lean towards the 9. From the point of view of the 9, the environment is less threatening; harmony, the ability to listen and gain more understanding become more accessible. It is partly through their social developments and internal openness that Shell was able to take a step in the right direction.

An active attempt to change the Enneagram typology of an organization can rarely be achieved

without damage. I have myself observed how a Type 1 organization thought they should become more like successful 3 organizations in their sector. A lot of effort was put into an attempt to change the image of the company, with the result that the core energy of the organization, their superior quality, slowly disappeared. And it was precisely the employees who felt most connected to the company who were then those who left it.

Are there any interesting commercial applications for the Enneagram?

Some time ago, one of my clients, the director of a large consultancy who was very familiar with the Enneagram, told me the following story. He had been invited to make a proposal to an important potential client, in competition with several other consultancies. The director knew the six members of the Board of his potential client company quite well. He knew them well enough to have a fair idea of their probable enneagram-types. After establishing the framework for his proposal, he drew up six different proposals in the same vein, adapting the word choice and style of each version to the enneagram-type of each board member. For Type 6, he emphasized the reliability of the approach to be used in the project, while for Type 8, it was the high impact of the project that was highlighted a little more. The Board was impressed with his proposal and decided to award him the order.

Such applications of the Enneagram naturally require appropriate care in use, even if only to inform the client about the different emphases in the proposals. But apart from that, something happened here that occurs in every service-oriented activity, namely an attempt to speak the language of the client —without neglecting the truth in the process, of course. Just as it is helpful to be able to speak French to a French-Canadian and Spanish to a Chilean, it is useful to speak to people in a way that allows them to understand our message clearly. In fact, we continually need to adapt to our customers, and the Enneagram can be used to optimize the situation.

3

Working with the Enneagram

This chapter provides the answers to the following questions:

- How do people recognize their type?
- How can I find out what type someone else is?
- How does a typing interview work?
- What is an example of a particularly complicated typing interview?
- What is the use of panel interviews in workshops?
- To what extent does the panel contribute to the development of knowledge about the Enneagram?
- Is the panel another way of finding out what type you are not?

How do people recognize their type?

There are people who pick out their type immediately when they hear or read about the enneagram-types. Others find a workshop or typing session helpful. Still others work on the subject for months before they recognize which type is theirs. Once in a while, someone will revise his or her choice after a period of time. In the course of my own Enneagram training, one of my colleagues had a sudden insight just before the examination that put her on the trail of a different type from the one she had believed to apply years earlier. Her willingness to continue her self-assessment in this way had an inspiring and also thought-provoking effect.

My experience in workshops is that about half of the participants have settled on a preferred type after about two hours. A quarter hesitates between two different options, and the final quarter needs more time to come to a conclusion. Of those who make a fast choice, about 20% revise their choice during the course of the workshop. By the end of the workshop, almost everyone has a clear picture of his or her own type. Once in a while, I get a phone-call later from someone who has arrived at a different conclusion later.

How can I find out what another person's type is?

It is not easy to type someone else precisely. That is perhaps a good thing. Some managers, co-workers or colleagues can easily be recognized from the descriptions, but even then, caution is recommended. After all, how well do we really know someone, to be certain of being able to make a correct assessment? We often notice how difficult it is to define our own type, never mind that of someone else. My suggestion is therefore not to concern ourselves too much with the discovery of someone else's type. What can be useful is to notice their behavior and our own reaction to it. We could then ask ourselves whether the other person shows certain characteristics that remind us of a particular type. For instance, we might notice that an important client reacts quickly and directly to our suggestions. We recognize these traits as belonging to types 3, 7 and 8. Of course, we don't know with certainty that the person is a 3, 7 or 8, but on the basis of our knowledge of the Enneagram, we know the patterns of behavior that are likely to apply to some types rather than others.

There are other links that make some aspects of the different types more easily recognizable. One way is to consider the manner in which different types communicate. A review of this would bring you to the following descriptions.

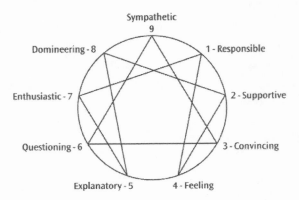

You could also consider how the types handle conflict.

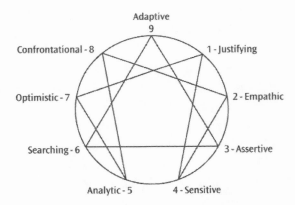

A further clue is provided by considering what it is that the different types avoid,

or what they appear to seek.

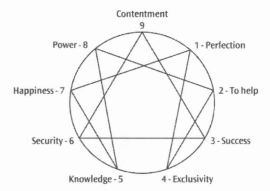

If you use these indicators, it is advisable first of all to answer which of the above mentioned themes apply to the other person, and then to consider what the Enneagram has to say about it. Recognition of certain aspects does not yet mean that the person is indeed that type, but it does provide a basis for further study.

How does a typing interview work?

The typing interview examines which type best applies to the interviewee. The interview is usually part of a typing session. A session of this kind usually lasts for two hours, with the interview in the first hour. The second half of the session is dedicated to a discussion of the findings from the interview. Questions relating to all nine types are asked in the course of the interview. If I am holding the interview myself, I usually ask first how the person thinks others see him. This is in fact the same question I presented to the reader at the beginning of this book. I ask what they think those who know them best appreciate in them, and what they find difficult. The reply to this question can already help point in the direction of one or more types. At least as important as the content of the answers is the way in which the question is answered. Body posture, voice and facial expression can give a lot of information about the enneagram-type.

The interviewer

Another important indicator is my own experience when I am talking to someone. If I get the feeling that I, as the interviewer, am not doing my job well enough, that may be an indication of a Type 1 perspective on the part of my client. It would certainly be useful in this case to enquire further into 1 aspects. Sometimes I feel supported by the client. It is as if he is doing his best to put me at ease. In that case it would make sense to enquire further into Type 2 characteristics. I may also get the feeling that I'm not going fast enough. This could indicate a type 3 subject who is somewhat impatient. A potential sign of recognition of a 4 could be when the interviewee directly or indirectly tries to ascertain how I experience certain things myself. I might also get a sense that I shouldn't enquire too deeply into personal matters—a sign of a possible Type 5. It may be that I am somewhat confused by the client, because on the one hand I feel criticized and on the other hand I seem to be supported, and sometimes he appears to contradict himself. This can be an indication that the other person is a 6. When I feel inspired to talk about all sorts of interesting but inessential matters, it could be that I'm talking to a 7. It can also happen that I get the feeling that I have to be very direct in order to hold the other person's attention, pointing in the direction of an 8. When I feel comfortable, but experience myself as a little lacking in energy, the indications encourage further investigation into the possibility that I have a Type 9 in front of me.

An interviewer tries to remain in as neutral a position as possible, in order to be as receptive as possible to both verbal and non-verbal signals. This is in fact the attitude we all assume to varying degrees when we are listening attentively to someone else.

Jumping to conclusions

It is important that the interviewer is aware of all this and at the same time does not allow himself to draw premature conclusions. Anyone who has held a selection interview knows how difficult this can be. There is a huge temptation to make a decision based on first impressions, and it often appears to be difficult to rid oneself of the first impression. The same is true of typing sessions. I have often quickly had an impression of a possible type. The art then lies in not allowing myself to be too attached to this impression. It could turn out that the impression occurred because the interviewee reminded me of someone else whose type I already know. Closer investigation may reveal my error. If I had no opportunity to interview him, I could run the risk of typing a person on the basis of incorrect information.

Specific questions are asked of each type. For Type 3, some of the questions will concern the experience of success and failure. It is useful to ask a Type 6 about doubt and security. Ultimately, the point is to unearth sufficient information in order to be able to exclude eight of the nine options.

An interviewer will notice that the conversation flows more easily with questions that are applicable to the type. The subject finds it easier to place the questions and usually answers them in a more lively and colorful manner. Just as with a panel that often fills the whole room with the atmosphere and specific qualities that belong to their type, the type of an interviewee also becomes more visible when his own type is under discussion. Often, although not always, the atmosphere takes on his specific qualities, as it were. This can be particularly interesting when the situation is seen as an incentive towards continued self-assessment.

Difficult circumstances

Broadly speaking, there are two situations that can make it particularly difficult to determine a type. In the first instance, the client may have little or no ability for self-reflection. This is essential in order to be able to answer questions about ourselves. If we simply don't know how we stand in relation to success, fear or anger, it is indeed difficult to answer any questions about it. The less self-knowledge there is, the more difficult it is to establish a typology. Of course, this is applicable for more than the typing interview. With a limited level of self-awareness, it is also difficult to answer a questionnaire. Generally speaking, the ability for self-reflection and therefore self-knowledge increases over the years. When this ability is actively developed through training and coaching, the pace of the process is usually considerably increased. Given that most organizations pay at least some attention to the development of personal effectiveness and leadership skills through training and coaching, the ability for self-reflection is generally reasonably well developed.

The second situation that can make it difficult to determine the enneagram-type is paradoxically enough, a high level of personal development. The enneagram-type could be compared to a rough diamond. During the course of our lives, we learn from experience to polish our character as best as we can. We get wiser about restraining some aspects of our personality, and knowing which qualities it would be good to develop. It is this polishing activity that refines our personality. Looking for the type is like looking for the rough diamond. The more someone has developed, the more difficult this is. For example, if you ask a probable Type 8 how he feels about confrontation, you could expect him to say something along the lines of it being "an interesting way to get to know people better". If the reply is "I don't like it, because I notice how it can upset the relationship", this will not immediately be reminiscent of an 8. In actual fact, it does not exclude the possibility that he is an 8 who really finds confrontation interesting. He may have discovered from experience that his approach to confrontation can lead to disruption of his relationships. He has learned to count to ten in the face of a possible confrontation, and benefited from the exercise. In this situation it is important for the interviewer to enquire into the past, with a question like "I understand that you don't like confrontation now. Has this always been the case?" If he is an 8, he is likely to tell us how he used to deal with confrontation differently, but has now learned better and will only react as he used to do in extreme circumstances. In other words, he has learned from the past, but that does not mean that the impulse has changed. As in the example of crossing your arms, there is a good chance that this 8 has learned that it can be to his advantage to cross his arms the other way around sometimes. This is the phenomenon that we often term 'learning', 'wisdom', 'experience', or 'maturity'; i.e., not acting on impulse but according to what is seen to be sensible.

You might ask whether this person is therefore still an 8. But if you ask what this person considers to be the most natural, it is the characteristics of the type that are named. It is furthermore my experience that even in the case of presumably very developed individuals, questions about difficult situations with other people at work and in private life usually reveal situations that are still related to the original type.

To summarize, the more someone has optimized his personal effectiveness, the more difficult it can be discover the right type in a short space of time.

The paradox of the typing interview

A typing interview has something paradoxical about it. One of the nicest aspects of the Enneagram is the search process. The integrity of the search is most optimally guaranteed when someone comes to his own conclusions. A typing interview may place the responsibility for the search outside the person himself. The second half of the session is therefore mainly a discussion of the findings. If the client holds a different opinion from the interview, it is the client's view that takes precedence. In order to stimulate the search, I often advise people to investigate their own possible type first, for example by reading a book about it or attending a workshop. If doubts then remain, a typing session can be helpful.

In team workshops where we work with the Enneagram, we usually hold a typing session before the start of the workshop. The reason for this is that a faulty Enneagram typing can lead to unnecessary complications within the team. Good preparatory research can prevent this from happening.

Have you an example of a particularly complicated typing interview?

I once held a typing interview with a Japanese manager within the framework of a team session with the management team of a Dutch multinational company. He was a senior manager within the company and had been posted to The Netherlands for a few years. Until then, I had had no experience of the Japanese culture. It was extremely difficult to determine the extent to which the answers to questions and his manner of answering them had to do with his own typology, or with his internalization of Japanese cultural characteristics. In the course of the interview, I began to ask him if he could give me an indication of how other Japanese might answer the different questions. For example, his answer to the question as to whether he often became angry was no. But when I asked him to compare himself with most Japanese, he replied that he thought that other Japanese would probably think that he was often angry.

It was difficult to come to a definitive conclusion. The point here is that it is important to make a difference between personal motivation and the cultural influence.

How do you use panel interviews in your workshops?

The methodology of the panel interviews as I use them is based on the way in which Helen Palmer developed the method. Simply said, people of the same typology are asked to come forward and participate in a panel. It is a bit like a talk show, in which the interviewer holds a discussion with the guests and the audience sits to one side to listen to the discussion. The interviewer asks the panel to talk about the issues that arise for their particular group. This often leads to extensive replies with illustrative examples. It is important for the interviewer to listen attentively and non-judgmentally. The involvement is often so strong that both the audience and the interviewer can get the feeling that they themselves are becoming the same type. Participants in the room not only receive factual information about the type, they also get a good feeling for a number of other aspects that belong to the type that can be read between the lines through their way of expressing themselves. This latter point is a fascinating experience. Some types have more energy than others, for example. So when the 9 panel begins, some of the audience start to fade. With the 8 panel, the audience is more likely to feel shaken to attention. Some types are more oriented towards themselves, others towards the audience. The 7 panel will mainly focus on having a good time, while the 3 panel will probably more or less want to impress their listeners. An enneagram-type is like a piece of music. We may get an impression of the music from the score and the lyrics, but we have to hear the song first to really get the feel of it. The enneagram-type works the same way. As a listener, you not only acquire knowledge; you also start to develop a feel for the different types after a while. On the other side, the members of the panel often acquire more clarity for themselves through talking to others of their type about common points of recognition. This can be a very personal exchange. The enneagram-type is after all not only about our good points, but also particularly about the issues that we find difficult and which touch us deeply. One of the ways to protect the panel against possible judgments that other participants may have is to allow no discussion with the panel, simply listening to them carefully. Experience shows that when everyone has had their turn, there is not only more understanding for each other, but also more possibilities are seen about how to get along with each other.

To what extent does the panel contribute to the development of knowledge about the Enneagram?

The interesting aspect of the panel method is that it is not the Enneagram theory that drives it, but the anecdotes than the panel members have to tell. The work of a workshop facilitator is based on reliance on the panel as the experts about their own type, not in checking up on whether they meet certain conditions in order to be that type. From this point of view, because it is the panel members who know the facts, this is also an excellent way for the facilitator to acquire more knowledge about the types. The examples of the different types mentioned in this book are based on several thousands of anecdotes that I have heard from managers and professionals on panels over the years. The Enneagram is therefore neither more than less than a framework, allowing information about human incentives and motivation to be accumulated.

For this reason, anyone reading several books about the Enneagram will notice that the theory in the different books is more or less the same, but the examples and emphases may differ considerably.

Is the panel another way of finding out what type you are not?

Yes indeed, and this can operate in two ways. When a specific panel has the floor, you might feel like you're hearing yourself speak. This might not even have to do with the content of their answers, but the way in which they answer. It is also possible for someone to take their place on a panel, only to discover that he doesn't feel comfortable with the way in which his co-panelists are answering the questions. This could indicate that he not the type he originally thought himself to be.

4

The Enneagram and Personal Development

This chapter provides the answers to the following questions:

- What advantage is it to me as a manager to know my type?
- Has the Enneagram, and personal development in general, more to do with personal insight or changing behavior?
- How can the Enneagram help with coaching?
- I understand that the nine enneagram types originally developed as survival strategies and later became our strategies for success, with all their limitations. But how should I now see survival?
- What might be the incentives for deep personal change?
- What other suggestions are there for personal development, apart from the enneagram-type?

What advantage is it to me as a manager to know my type?

The most practical way of working with the Enneagram is to consult it when confronted with challenging issues at work or in your private life. Where there is conflict, for example, it is always useful to look at the issues for our own type and examine our behavior in this situation. It can also be useful to speculate about the possible types of the others involved, in order to see what challenges they entail for us. We can then adapt our approach accordingly. Talking the situation through with

someone can help to become more aware of our own behavior. It is useful to review what was said later, relating it to our knowledge of the
Enneagram and possibly using it to establish areas requiring attention.
Doing this repeatedly in difficult situations helps to broaden our range
of behavioral options.

**Has the Enneagram, and personal development in general, more to
do with personal insight or changing behavior?**

Both. Different behavior will not persist without insight. And if
insight does not lead to a change, then it is of little value. Let me give
you an example. A manager taking part in a leadership course using the
Enneagram comes to the conclusion that he is a Type 8. Type 8 is not a
good listener, so he learns listening skills. He then takes the time to 'listen' to people, but still thinks that his opinion is the only correct one.
It's unlikely that his new skills will last very long. In this example, the
person in question does in fact decide on his Enneagram type and
acquire certain new skills. However, no insight occurred as to why these
skills might be important. He had no experience to show him how he
was missing out and perhaps underestimating others, by not listening
properly. Without this kind of insight, it is difficult to bring about
changes in our behavior.

At the other end of the spectrum is the manager who returns to the
office after the same training course, telling his colleagues enthusiasti-
cally that he knows now that he is a Type 5 and finally understands why
his colleagues find him distant at times. He also understands why co-
workers do not always feel that he supports them, and even what his
wife means when she says that he keeps himself to himself too much.
These are very valuable insights, but of course the question is, what
consequences will these insights have for his behavior in future? If there
is no answer to this question, there is still some homework to be done.

How can the Enneagram help with coaching?

There are different definitions of coaching. One of the aims of coaching may be to help people to become more effective in the workplace. This is often not a question of acquiring expertise in terms of knowledge of the content of the work, but the ability to communicate effectively. Coaching sessions can help managers and professionals to become more aware of who they are, what they do, and what effects they have on their environment. The Enneagram is an excellent method of acquiring more insight into your own strengths and weaknesses. It also shows what the effect of them can be on others. And things really become interesting when a client is able to describe the important personages in his working environment in such a way that it becomes possible to conclude which enneagram-types they might be. The next step would be to look at what various situations offer in the way of opportunities to learn. When I carry out coaching projects myself, learning about the Enneagram almost always helps my client realize his goals. One of our first sessions is always dedicated to a typing interview. It is quite amazing, if no longer surprising, how the client's initial questions are usually closely related to the issues of his specific enneagram-type.

Whether as line manager, human resources consultant or in other functions, knowledge of the Enneagram helps a manager to become more effective as a coach. One of the biggest traps for a coach is to think that what works for us, must work for someone else. In fact, we are usually not even aware that the advice we are giving others is actually what we would tell ourselves in the same situation. The Enneagram shows clearly how all types have different points of view, and that they are at their best when approached in their own way. Think of the enneagram-types as different languages; there is usually little point in speaking Dutch to a Frenchman, for example. To coach him effectively, we need to understand the French language and be able to speak it well enough to build up an effective relationship.

The Enneagram also indicates that coaching skills must be adapted to the situation. If a coach has learned to listen attentively and not interrupt, he may make a good impression on some people. However, the coach will be more effective if he interrupts and makes his own opinion known to the 8. And a Type 9 will appreciate the coach's listening skills, but may well need to have more structure brought into the discussion.

The Enneagram may also bring the qualities and weak spots of the coach to light. The Type 9 coach will presumably have no difficulty listening, but can he be directive when necessary, and set limits when the situation calls for it? The 6 coach may be good at asking questions, but runs the risk of making a mountain out of a molehill. The 5 coach is likely to be good at analysis, but the question is whether he can show empathy when that is what is needed. Type 8 is able to motivate people, but occasionally leaves them little room to maneuver. In short, the Enneagram not only helps to clarify projections that the coach may be making—'it works for me, so it should work for him'—it also helps avoid the failings and build on the qualities of his specific type, in his role as coach.

I understand that the nine enneagram-types originally developed as survival strategies and later became our strategies for success, with all their limitations. But how should I now see survival?

The physical survival of children in the Western world is no longer under threat, generally speaking. Apart from tragedies like mortal illness, accident or war, not many people die of starvation in this part of the world. Our survival strategies now have more to do with psychological survival. Psychological survival requires love. The Enneagram could be seen as nine different ways of getting love.

Type 1 assumes that being loved is dependent on the degree to which he knows exactly how things should be done, and doing them perfectly. Type 2 believes he will be loved as long as he helps others. Type 3 assumes that the love to be received is related to the performance he delivers. Type 4's experience is that he must be special and unique in order to be loved. Type 5 thinks that being loved has to do with being knowledgeable and understanding the importance of things. Type 6 decides that love is available only if he is sure about things, or when the environment offers him the security that he can't find in himself. For Type 7, love is connected with pleasure and avoidance of pain. The 8 tries to get love by being powerful and exercising control. Type 9 learns that love is available as long as the surroundings are harmonious.

All strategies work in their own way, but we are underestimating ourselves by identifying with any strategy. Yet identification is an unavoidable psychological mechanism, as illustrated by the metaphor of the circle, the trauma and the fortress. At the beginning, we experience unity through the circle. There is no difference between us and the world. The inside and the outside world are the same. This is and understandable standpoint for the consciousness of a baby in the womb. But when earthly life begins, the concept can't be maintained. If we continue to identify with the circle, it is impossible to survive. We have to learn to relate to our surroundings. Enter duality. Now there appears to be a separation between me and the other. Being left behind in the supermarket is a metaphor for the experience of this separation that we call trauma. In point of fact, separation occurs without being left behind in a supermarket; this is simply intended to clarify the mechanism. When the child discovers that he and his mother are no longer one, but are separate individuals, this creates a wound by definition. The reason for the fortress is so as not to have to feel the wound.

When a particular strategy works in winning the love we experienced when everything was still one, we believe that we come in contact with that early feeling of oneness. In fact, no matter how much we try, our environment can never give us back that feeling. The longing for love from our environment can't fill the hole in the circle; we alone can do that for ourselves. And that can only happen when we realize that by attempting to get love from outside, we are denying something in ourselves. The pain or frustration that we experience though insufficient love from the environment is actually the pain of having lost contact with our own essence. We lost contact with our essence when we decided to identify ourselves, as it were, with the strategy, the fortress, rather than with our own essence, the circle itself. If we really see this, it becomes obvious that our true face has more to do with the circle of essence than with the fortress that is our enneagram-type.

For many of us, no matter how much self-exploration we have done, we repeatedly seem to choose identification with the survival strategy in difficult situations, and it often takes the upper hand again. Few people seem to realize absolute freedom from this identification. But that is no reason for not wanting to achieve it for ourselves.

What might be the incentives for deep personal change?

Deep personal change is no easy matter. As far as I have been able to discover, there are five incentives for active change: pain, acceptance, longing, emotion or coincidence. The jargon for the result of these incentives is transformation, meaning a sort of chemical process, something irreversible.

Before examining this further, we must remember that some changes in human development happen by themselves. People change over time, just as trees acquire another ring each year. For children, this is evident in their physical growth. In terms of human development, we acquire knowledge and experience. Blossom appears on the trees. As people, we blossom by developing our talents and in a sense, becoming more beautiful because of them. The trees bear fruit. From the point of view of human development, this is the phase in which we contribute to the world through the work we do or by meaning something to other people. These are natural processes of change that in principle happen by themselves, just like the growth and blossoming of a tree. As long as the tree gets enough water and sunshine, and no damage occurs through being unnecessarily transplanted or having its branches cut off, the tree develops its potential all by itself. The same is true for people. If certain basic conditions are fulfilled and we don't experience excessive damage, the process of growth, blossoming and bearing fruit happens more or less by itself. The previously mentioned incentives are separate from the natural process of change described here.

Pain as an incentive for change

Pain is the most recognizable incentive for change. It does not always lead to change; indeed, it can also lead to temporary or definitive stagnation. In times of crisis, there is always an experience of pain. The Chinese sign for crisis consists of two symbols, one signifying danger and the other 'positive opportunity'. Anyone who has been through a mid-life crisis knows both of these aspects. The assumption used to be, as the phrase also suggests, that this was a crisis that occurred in the middle of our lives, around the age of forty. Early dreams have been fulfilled by then. We have a good job, a nice house, a wife and family, and yet we're still not really happy. Where to go from here? Because of the wider dynamics of present-day life, I have observed that the symptoms we used to label as mid-life crises can occur at all ages. In recent years I have had clients in my practice who were barely thirty, who had already reached the top of their career, had their first divorce behind them and were asking themselves what else there was to life. Others are long past forty before they begin to feel the need for serious reflection on their work and life in general, stimulated by the same issues. The pain caused by divorce or loss of any kind can open our eyes to what is really important, and has the potential for bringing us closer to ourselves. This type of crisis often seems to provide a strong incentive for personal insight and awareness of our own behavior.

Pain, however uncomfortable, can help to open our eyes further to the effect that our behavior has on ourselves and our surroundings, and therefore lead to growth and change. From the point of view of the Enneagram, it is often the negative aspects of our type that become most clearly apparent in crisis situations. The 3 may conclude that he only ever had time for prestige and status and lacked sensitivity for his environment. The 9 may come to the conclusion that the real problem was that he had lost sight of his own needs.

When people experience little or no pain, the incentive for self-reflection and change is often less. This means that it is not always easy to create successful management development programs. Young talent at the top has generally had little experience of personal crises. Obviously, crises take time and energy that leave less room for fast career development. If a change of address or the death of a grandmother are the worst disasters that have happened to date, it is unlikely that these events will have triggered important insights that could help the manager to recognize his own potential. In such instances, it is often more useful to work with the actual problems that he is struggling with in the work situation, because it is here that opportunities for him to learn often lie hidden.

Getting to know our enneagram-type can be painful, since it confronts us with sides of ourselves that we had not yet seen or wanted to see. This pain can be the incentive for further investigation. Closer examination can lead to more understanding for our situation, which allows the pain to ease.

Longing as an incentive for change

Longing can also be an important source of inspiration leading to change. Longing to develop our potential is important and necessary if we are also to actually do it. Someone who says that he just 'is the way he is and there's nothing to be done about it', would appear to have little inclination to develop his untapped potential. Or at least, his longing is buried deep. Learning one's own type can awaken or increase the desire to develop our own potential.

Acceptance as an incentive for change

Aside from pain and longing, acceptance of the current reality can also be an important incentive for change. If we really face up to who we are, with all of our qualities and our limitations, acceptance occurs and with it, relaxation. Facing up to who we are requires the courage of looking truth in the eye. It takes courage and also the ability to see the truth as it is, neither more nor less, neither more colorful nor more gray than the reality. The truth will set you free, it is said, and that's a fact. If we really look at ourselves without minimizing our failings or talents, there is peace, and this brings about change. We don't need to pretend to be someone we are not; we are more ourselves. Subtle though this may be, this might be the most fundamental change that can happen. Identification with the enneagram-type becomes less prominent. It was after all primarily a façade, and those in our environment begin to find us more authentic, more ourselves, when we no longer hold it up. Experiences of pain and longing often precede this process of change.

Emotion as an incentive for change

Deep emotion can also lead to change. We may be moved by nature or beautiful music. It is also possible to be deeply moved by another person. Someone may embody something that we experience as authentic, which allows us to come into contact with an authentic dimension of ourselves that we had never before been aware of. Being moved by something or someone outside of ourselves touches something in us that may no longer have been activated, but it was always there—otherwise we would not been touched. We speak of being moved by something outside of ourselves, but in fact we are touched by something inside that resonates with the outside world. Experiences of deep emotion can therefore help us to become more aware of our previously untapped potential, and our recognition of different aspects helps us to integrate them in ourselves. Because it is usually easier to let ourselves be touched by people rather than by a stone, for instance, others can often be of help to us. A Type 1 may be moved by contact with another Type 1, for example, because through recognition of his authenticity or his complete perfection, he feels supported in developing these aspects further.

Coincidence as an incentive for change

No matter how positive our attitude towards change and development, we seldom consciously take genuinely far-reaching steps, yet they nevertheless seem to happen sometimes. We often call this coincidence, serendipity or synchronicity. We take on a new job because it seems to be interesting and challenging, but had no way of knowing that there would be so much to learn, or that so much courage would be needed to achieve satisfactory results. The following anecdote is one I have come across in various versions over the years.

Long ago there was a rich Dutchman who lived in the Dutch East
Indies. He had made his fortune by upping his roots and moving to the
East Indies as an entrepreneur. Once there, he had bought up planta-
tions and become a celebrated and above all very wealthy businessman.
His fortune brought him not only land, ships, factories and a great deal
of gold, but also close relationships with very highly situated people all
over the world. One day, he decided to organize a big party on one of his
country estates. The estate was of unimaginable circumference and
beauty, and next to the main pavilion there was also a large lake. The
party took place on the banks of the lake. Row upon row of servants
stood ready to serve the guests on the terraces around the lake with the
most wonderful delicacies to eat and drink. When all the guests had
arrived, among them some very important people, the host expressed
his happiness that everyone had come to the party. He told them that he
had a reason for giving this feast. He explained how, during the course
of his successful life, people with the quality of courage had always
greatly impressed him, and that there was nothing he would rather do
than dedicate this party to them. That was why he had chosen to fill the
lake for this event—and it was a very large lake—with hundreds of
crocodiles. Impressed as he was by courageous people, he proposed that
the first of the guests to swim across the lake would be rewarded with
everything he could possibly wish for. Estates, gold, access to important
people; even his own beautiful daughter would become the possessions
of the successful candidate. At these words, a ripple of excitement ran
through the crowd. Only a gentle murmur was heard as they seated
themselves at the tables and began their meal. Suddenly, a loud splash
was heard from the lake. All the guests turned to look, their gaze fixed
on one of their number who had meanwhile reached the center of the
lake. The crocodiles, until now lying quietly in the water, were visibly
agitated and began to move with increasing interest in the direction of
their potential prey. The guest swimming in the lake was the beautiful
wife of one of the most popular of the guests, swam for her life.

Meanwhile, all of the other guests had gathered at the edge of the lake. The crocodiles, appearing to favor their chances, snapped wildly at the swimmer. For a moment it seemed that one of them snatched the white dress of his imminent prey in its teeth, but in some mysterious way she escaped. With unbelievable will power, she crossed the final stretch of water and climbed unhurt out of the water. The host, deeply impressed by this courageous act, ran towards the heroine to congratulate her on this incredible feat. He repeated what he had said before, that she should have everything she could possible wish for that it was in his power to give. But before he had finished speaking, the woman interrupted him. She said she thought it was wonderful that she was to be rewarded for her performance, but first of all, who was the bastard who pushed her into the water?

It is often not the conscious choice of a courageous act that causes us to change, but life itself that gives us the push.

What other suggestions are there in the area of personal development, apart from the Enneagram type?

To answer this question properly, we first need to clarify what is really meant by the term development. The literal meaning of the word is to bring out that which has been enveloped or not yet exposed. Something that has not been exposed has been in the dark. Development therefore means bringing light to the situation. Development is therefore not so much a case of learning something new, but lightening up or clearing away whatever prevents us from seeing our essence. This can often be seen with someone who is highly developed. Such a person inspires us because we experience them as authentic, or have the feeling that he is entirely himself and that all of his qualities have become visible. This inspiration could be seen as a suggestion that the same potential is hidden in us.

Another way of saying this is that development is nothing other than getting to know ourselves as we really are.

Feedback

There are two useful methods of approaching personal development. The key word for both methods is self-examination. The first approach is to gather information about ourselves through others. The second approach is to gather information about ourselves in ourselves. The question is whether there are methods that can help us to know ourselves better.

The first approach that may help here is based on the thought that learning occurs through developing awareness about the effect that our behavior has on others. In fact there are two ways to become aware of this. The first way is to take a good look at ourselves and the influence we have on others in our environment. This is not easy. I have found that when you ask team members to describe the intentions and behavior of their colleagues, they are able to do this unusually clearly and adequately. When it comes to describing themselves however, it's a different matter. Understandably so. It is harder to see ourselves than it is to see others. We have to go and stand in front of a mirror to be able to see our own face as easily as we can see the face of someone we are talking to. And when it comes to listening, you will notice that it is not easy to listen to yourself at the same time as you are speaking. We become accustomed to being who we are—we've lived with ourselves since we were born, after all—so it is no easy matter to arrive at an objective view. We take who we are to be a known fact, and don't usually ask any specific questions about it.

This is quite the opposite of what happens when faced with someone else; for example, when interviewing a candidate for a subordinate position. We pay careful attention to the candidate's behavior and character, and ask him some critical questions. We might notice that he talks slowly and never seems to waste his words. It may come to our attention that he looks away when asked certain questions, or stares at us a bit too intently. In short, we carry out a critical examination of him. For personal development, critical examination is necessary. Most of us have not learned this discipline. We generally tend to do it only in times of crisis, when we've lost a job or are faced with divorce. We then draw certain conclusions from the experience and then go back to normal relatively quickly. Interestingly, most people find the lessons they learn at such times to be useful and informative. But if you were to compare this with the functioning of a continuously running factory, it would be like not carrying out maintenance as part of a continuous quality control system; postponing repairs until the factory came to a grinding halt.

One good way to carry out our own maintenance is by developing better methods of self-observation. The ability to observe ourselves is like a diagnostic meter in a factory: it indicates the state of the processes being carried out. Methods like the Enneagram help us to access more measuring instruments in our own human factory. But because self-observation is difficult, the help of others is indispensable for most of us. It is for this reason that many of the development suggestions in this book include exercises that involve asking others for input. Learning how others experience us increases our chance of gathering information we couldn't see for ourselves, or of confirming assumptions we had made about ourselves.

However, as we know from science, there is no such thing as pure research: the perceiver also influences the results of the examination. The thermometer that is put into water to measure the temperature affects the temperature of the water itself, and by definition therefore cannot make a precise measurement. The same mechanism operates to a much greater extent when we ask others to evaluate our behavior. He, the perceiver, cannot make a precise discrimination, because his perception is colored by the instrument, i.e., the perceiver himself. There's interference on the line. In science, this problem is more or less compensated for by application of the law of larger numbers: If a large series of observations point in the same direction, it is reasonable to assume that the findings contain a high level of correctness. The same principle can be applied to our own development. So it is useful to get regular feedback about our behavior. If we get feedback that we can't place, it could be because it says more about the other person than us, or we are hearing something that is true, but new to us: we didn't know that yet, or perhaps didn't want to know. But it is possible that feedback will tell us something about ourselves as well as the other person. When this happens, it can be particularly useful to apply the law of large numbers, and extend our research to several people.

All things being equal, regular feedback will keep us attentive to the effect of our behavior and help us to adjust it. Practice of this kind also improves our ability to observe our own behavior, so that we will increasingly be aware of what we are doing and avoiding, even without feedback from others. Partly based on experience gained within human resources management, most organizations have reasonably functional feedback mechanisms. Regular functional and assessment discussions are a good example of this. Systems like 360-degree feedback clearly show how useful it can be to gather feedback from one's leaders as well as colleagues and co-workers.

Self-observation

A second approach towards personal development is an internal examination of how we orient our attention. This approach has not specifically been discussed in this book, but it is at least as interesting and useful as getting feedback from the environment. As I mentioned in the introduction, one of the reasons that it is difficult to change our behavior is because we usually run on automatic pilot, more than we want to or believe we do. The reason is that we are not aware that there is a moment of choice between an impulse and the action. In the introduction, this is compared with the way in which we automatically cross our arms, without thinking first whether, and if so, what the different ways are of doing this. It is only when we are aware of how and when an impulse arises that could lead to a specific action, that we are in a position to vary our repertory.

The Enneagram shows that the source of differences between people is not so much in their behavior, but in the different ways in which different types orient their attention. The automatic way in which attention is oriented does indeed lead to a certain range of behavior, but the source of this behavior is the way each type orients his attention. This explains why some types apparently demonstrate contradictory behavior, while others appear to show considerable similarities, even though their behavior is motivated by completely different incentives. Awareness of the way in which our attention is oriented is therefore essential in order to become freer of its influence on our behavior. It is not easy to see this. It is like waking someone up in the middle of the night and asking him what is most important to him. From the point of view of the Enneagram, Type 1 might say "How I can be perfect", Type 2, "How I can help", Type 3 might say "How I can be successful", and so on.

The most obvious way to observe our own thinking is to make a difference between that which is observed and the observer by internalizing, as it were, the eyes of the outsider as described in the previous approach. This apparently artificial splitting of ourselves enables us to allow our usual feelings and thoughts to occur and observe them at the same time. This is in fact what is meant by self-observation. Everyone with the habit of self-reflection will recognize the phenomenon. When we tell a loved one about the events of our day, we are able to do this because we can see what we have done, and remember what we experienced. It is more difficult to reflect on what is actually happening in the moment, rather than what has already happened. But it is possible. We can experience feelings and almost immediately express them. We have to be able to feel them and also observe them in order to be able to express them. The task becomes more difficult when we decide to observe all of the feelings and thoughts that occur, but not express them. The internal observer is then actively looking at the other part of the self that is not observing, but thinking and feeling. An interesting way of doing this is to close your eyes—so that you are less distracted by signals from the outside world—and pay attention to the thoughts and feelings that are occurring. We soon notice how quickly we become caught up in thoughts and feelings, and several seconds will pass in which we are unable to be there to observe. This is what usually happens in the course of our daily lives, without our being aware of it. If I were to ask you what your experience was ten minutes ago, you will quite probably not find it easy to remember. To do this exercise, it helps to count from one to ten with each breath, beginning again at one when you reach ten. Counting can help to active the inner observer.

In different spiritual traditions, exercises such as those described here—often called meditation—are seen as an essential discipline for development. Once we see how and when thoughts and feelings arise, we no longer need to be swayed by them against our will, and we can experience quietness and autonomy. In other words, by observing them, we are choosing to act on them or not. Only then can we talk about real freedom. Those interested in experimenting with this way of development could try the exercise described above for 15 minutes every day. Don't be discouraged when you notice how difficult it is to focus your attention on what you are doing. It takes most people years of training. In my opinion, development of the inner observer is at least as important as the first-mentioned approach. After all, it is only when we have developed the ability to observe ourselves with focused concentration that we are in a position to act from choice, rather than fly on automatic pilot.

PART 3

BIBLIOGRAPHY

A large number of books about the Enneagram have appeared in recent years. Some of these books are described here. The purpose of this section of the book is to clarify what different books you can find to help you to adapt further examination of the Enneagram to your individual wishes. The list given here is not complete, but it will give you a good overview of the different approaches and application areas of the Enneagram.

The books mentioned here have been selected for various reasons. Some of them discuss additional theoretical aspects of the Enneagram. Others are interesting because of the area of application that is described, or the comparison that is made with other systems. Where possible, I have indicated what other language versions of the books are available. It is often easier to learn something new when we can study it in our own language.

Books

Addison, H.A., *The Enneagram and Kabbalah: Reading Your Soul*, Jewish Lights Pub., 1998, 176 pages, ISBN 1580230016.

Rabbi Howard Addison, inspired by his discovery of the Enneagram, decided to make a comparative study of the Jewish mystical tradition, the Kabbalah, in comparison with the Enneagram. This is a book well worth reading for anyone who is interested in both systems or likes to compare different systems.

Almaas, A.H., *Facets of Unity, The Enneagram of Holy Ideas,* Diamond
Books, 1999, 350 pages,
    ISBN 09367131443.

Almaas is the founder of the Diamond Approach, which integrates
psychological knowledge and spiritual awareness. This approach differ-
entiates between Essence and Personality. Essence is what we really are.
It precedes formation of the personality, and we have the potential of
becoming more deeply anchored in it. The personality develops in
order to protect Essence—as in the metaphor of the fortress described
earlier. Most writers about the Enneagram describe the limitations and
qualities of each Enneagram personality type, and the best way to deal
with them. Almaas takes a different angle. He shows us that a Holy Idea
lies at the source of each type, rather than talking about the types from
the point of view of the personality. A Holy Idea is a specific quality
arising from essence. As I mentioned in the first chapter, 'Pure Hope' or
'Pure Love', for example, are essential qualities. Almaas describes how,
when essence becomes snowed under, 'Pure Love' is distorted in a personality fixation on harmony.

This is an excellent book that takes the reader into the deeper dimen-
sions of the Enneagram. It demands serious attention, however. It is
more suitable as reading material on a sabbatical, than for quick perusal
in between other matters.

Baron, R. and E. Wagele, *The Enneagram made Easy: Discover the 9
Types of People,* Harper San Francisco, 1994, 176 pages, ISBN 0062510266.

A nice book, richly illustrated with drawings and cartoons, and
worth buying for that reason alone. A particularly amusing and illustrative cartoon shows the different types before and after a party. The personality inventory, intended to help the reader discover his own type,
can be misleading. Those familiar with the MBTI* will enjoy the chapter comparing it with the Enneagram.

Baron, R. and E. Wagele, *Are you my type, am I yours? Relationships made easy through the Enneagram,* Harper San Francisco, 1995, 192 pages, ISBN 006251248X.

Another agreeable and accessible book by Baron and Wagele, also illustrated with drawings and cartoons, looking at relationships between the different types. The book indicates the favorite types that different people choose for partner. The wife of a type 3 usually turns out to be a 1 or a 2, for example, while the female type 8 generally has a type 5, 6 or 9 husband. There is unfortunately no indication of the basis for these conclusions. The question of look-alikes is discussed, and comparisons again made with the MBTI (Myers Briggs Type Indicator).

Beesing, M., P.H. O'Leary and R.J. Nogosek, *The Enneagram, A Journey of Self Discovering,* Dimension Books, 1984, 223 pages, ISBN 0871932148.

I have never actually seen this book, but as far as is known, this is the first book every published about the Enneagram. Reason enough to mention it.

Condon, Th., *The Enneagram Movie and Video Guide: How to see Personality Styles in the Movies,* The Changeworks, 1994, out of print.

When Condon was sentenced to several months in hospital after an accident, he decided to create an invention out of necessity/turn a difficulty into a virtue. He watched hundreds of films and videos and typed the characters. The book has meanwhile become a little dated, but will still be a delight to film-lovers.

Frager, R. (editor), *Who am I, Personality Types of Self-Discovery,* Putnam Publishing Group, 1994, 267 pages, ISBN 0874777615.

Those interested in comparing different typologies will find this book worthwhile. Only some of the typologies that are used in organizations are included, but all the more unconventional approaches are reviewed. Various experts describe a total of about 20 typologies. Apart from the Enneagram, the Jungian thinking on which the MBTI* is based is examined. There is a discussion of Black and Mouton's meanwhile classic theory from which the concept of situational leadership was developed. Other approaches included in the book are Steiner's temperament categories, Lowen's bio-energetic structures, astrological typologies, the Ayurvedic typologies used by Chopra, and many others.

Goldberg, M., *Getting Your Boss's Number, and Many Other Ways to use the Enneagram at Work,* Metamorphous, 1996, 279 pages, ISBN 0062512986.

The title does not nearly do justice to the contents of this book. It is a very complete Enneagram book for managers and professionals. Leadership and communication are looked at from the point of view of the Enneagram. The author, an American management consultant, draws on his experience with the CIA and Motorola. His descriptions of organizations are worth reading. Motorola is defined as a 1, for example, Mary Kay Cosmetics as a 2, McDonalds as a 3, Ritz-Carlton as a 4, Mars as a 5, the CIA as a 6, 3M as a 7, Microsoft as an 8 and the US Postal Service as a 9. Goldberg also dedicates a chapter to the question of how the different types co-operate with each other.

Linden, A. and M. Spalding, *The Enneagram and NLP: a Journey of Evolution,* Metamorphous, 1994, out of print.

Linden and Spalding look at the Enneagram types in the light of a number of NLP concepts. They indicate which NLP interventions could lead to positive change for the different types.

Maitri, S., *The Spiritual Dimension of the Enneagram, Nine Facets of the Soul,* Tarcher Putman, 2000, 319 pages, ISBN 1585420174.

Together with A.H. Almaas and Helen Palmer, Sandra Maitri belongs to the group of people who were instructed in the enneagram by

Claudio Naranjo in the 1970s. The book is thorough, complete and profound. Like Almaas, with whom she has worked for many years, Maitri encourages the reader to look more closely at the personality and to see the enneagram type as a means of entering into closer contact with our essential nature. Readers hoping to determine their type with the help of the chapter on 'Determining your ennea-type' may feel that the information is somewhere inadequate. This apparent disadvantage is, however, generously compensated for by the rich and experienced manner in which the nine types are described in the rest of the book.

Palmer, H., The Enneagram, *Understanding Yourself and the Others in Your Life,* Harper San Francisco, 1991, 392 pages, ISBN 0062506838.

This is the first Enneagram book written by Helen Palmer. Among other things in her books, she draws on long experience with what she calls the oral tradition. The oral tradition prescribes that knowledge of the different types is best gained through giving the word to those who recognize themselves in each of the types. It is the anecdotes of people themselves, after all, that bring the types to life in all their diversity. Palmer's knowledge is therefore not so much based on theory, but on what the thousands of participants on panels in her workshops have actually said. Her books are largely based on these examples.

This book also gives a good historical background of the Enneagram, and an explanation of the spiritual concepts underlying the system. It is not always easy to read. Her following books are more accessible. Palmer's own explanation for this is that it was her first book. It has been a bestseller in the U.S.

Palmer, H., *The Enneagram in Love and Work: Understanding your Intimate & Business Relationships,* Harper San Francisco, 1996, 432 pages, ISBN 0062507214.

Palmer's second book, another bestseller. This book is more practical and offers somewhat less background information. In-depth focus is given to the dynamics of each type in work and personal relationships. Clear descriptions, again with many practical examples and good tips. Particularly the last part of the book is very useful. Here, Palmer gives an overview of opportunities and pitfalls of relationships between the different types. She indicates what the situation is in relationships between a 1 and another 1, a 2 and a 2, and so on. All possible combinations are examined, and a difference is made between working and personal relationships.

Palmer, H., *The Pocket Enneagram; Understanding the 9 Types of People,* Harper San Francisco, 1995, 96 pages, ISBN 0062513273.
This little book is a brief excerpt from Palmer's first book. The size is handy, but not suitable as an introduction to the Enneagram. It is too conceptual for this purpose and needs more explanation. For an advanced reader, the book is superfluous.

Palmer, H., and P.B. Brown, *The Enneagram Advantage: Putting the 9 Personality Types to Work in the Office,* Three Rivers Press, 1998, 304 pages, ISBN 0609802208.
In this book, Palmer and Brown focus entirely on how managers and professionals function. They discuss the different types on the basis of the themes of communication, motivation, time management, negotiating, and training and development. It is a practical and clear book with plenty of examples. A self-assessment quiz at the beginning of the book offers the reader the possibility of defining his own type.

Riso, D.R. and R. Hudson, *Personality Types: Using the Enneagram for Self-Discovery,* Houghton Mifflin Co., 1996, 515 pages, ISBN 0395798671.
Riso and Hudson, together with Palmer, are probably the most popular writers on the Enneagram in the U.S. In my view, the most important contribution made by Riso and Hudson is their categorization of different degrees of development for the different types. They define a

'healthy', an 'average' and an 'unhealthy' type. Each of these categories is sub-divided into three levels, so that you arrive at a reasonably, considerably or very healthy type. Nine levels of functioning altogether are examined for each type. It would be all too easy to situate an impossible boss or co-worker in the unhealthy category and define our favorite people as healthy, and this is of course the potential danger of this type of categorization. It not only encourages us to recognize patterns within the types, but also to judge their effectiveness. However, as with every system of classification, it can be very insightful when used with care.

Riso and Hudson use a different definition of the sub-types than most authors. They base their observations on the premise that a sub-type is formed through the influence of the neighboring type. The Type 6 influence by Type 5 therefore forms one sub-type, and the Type 6 influence by Type 7 forms another sub-type. The amount of diligence that Riso and Hudson dedicated to this work must have been huge, alone in assigning a name, not only to the sub-types, but to each of the 9 levels within a type. Type 8 at level 8, for instance, the second-lowest level, becomes the *Omnipotent Megalomaniac*. At level 2 he comes off considerably better, understandably enough, as the *Self-confident Person*.

Riso and Hudson also describe the movement along the lines from one type to another differently from the stress and relaxation points used by Palmer, defining these as the directions of integration and disintegration.

A voluminous book therefore, but absolutely worth studying. This is the only book on the Enneagram until now that is also available in a Japanese translation.

Riso, D.R. and R. Hudson, *The Wisdom of the Enneagram: the Complete Guide to Psychological and Spiritual Growth for the Nine Personality Types*, Bantam Doubleday Dell Pub., 1999, 400 pages, ISBN 0553378201.

Their most recent book. To be recommended for anyone who wishes to use the Enneagram for continued personal development. Incidentally, the authors no longer use their original concept of sub-types here, speaking instead of *wings*.

Rohr, R. and A. Ebert, *Discovering the Enneagram: An Ancient Tool for a New Spiritual Journey,* Crossroad Pub. Co., 1993, 255 pages, ISBN 0824511859.

The Franciscan Rohr and his Lutheran colleague Ebert give a clear and also in-depth picture of the Enneagram from a Christian point of view. This is an extremely accessible book, also for those with a non-Christian background. The book lends itself to repeated reading. Ebert and Rohr did not let themselves be distracted into trying to find nice names for the different types. The types are described according to what each one actually can't do without. For the 1 it is *the Need to be Perfect,* for the 2, *the Need to be Needed,* for the 3, *the Need to Succeed,* for the 4, *the Need to be Special,* for the 5, *the Need to Perceive,* for the 6, *the Need for Security/Certainty,* for the 7, *the Need to Avoid Pain,* for the 8, *the Need to be Against* and finally for the 9, *the Need to Avoid.*

Salmon, E., *ABC de l'Enneagramme,* Grancher ABC, 1997, 246 pages, ISBN 2733905422.

Until now, this is the only book about the Enneagram to have been written in French. It is a compact and playful introduction with a lot of cartoons. Particularly interesting is the chapter about the historical background. The reader is led in a simple way from Pythagoras up to the Enneagram, as we know it today.

Webb, K., *Principles of the Enneagram,* Thorsons Pub., 1996, 160 pages, ISBN 0722531915.

An introduction to the Enneagram that gives a clear overview. Karen Webb is a student of Helen Palmer and also derives her knowledge from the oral tradition. She bases her view on the premise that each type can be classified in three sub-types, each of which is described. She shows how different types resemble each other, the look-alikes, and how they can be differentiated.

Videos and cassettes

Palmer, H., *The Enneagram, Exploring the Nine Psychological Types and their Inter-Relationships in Love and Life,* Sounds True, audiocassette, ISBN 1564553132.

Six wonderful cassettes in which Palmer tells you everything you want to know about the Enneagram. They include recordings from workshops. A lively introduction, and if you listen to them in the car, you'll have heard them all in the space of a week.

Palmer, H., *Nine Points of View, Nine Men on Relationships,* Workshops in the Oral Tradition with Helen Palmer, 1994.

A video of nine interviews with the different types. These are not actors, but students of Helen Palmer talking about their types. It is interesting to notice differences in posture, facial expression, the way of speaking and dressing. Some people think the video a little slow, but all of the most important issues are discussed in it. Europeans will want to ensure that they get the Pal version of this video, as most European video recorders cannot use the American system.

Palmer, H., *Nine Points of View, Nine Women on Relationships,* Workshops in the Oral Tradition with Helen Palmer, 1994.

As above, except that it is the ladies' turn to speak.

Riso, D.R., *The Power of the Enneagram: a New Technology of Self-Discovery,* Simon & Schuster, ISBN 0671567977.

An introduction to the Enneagram. A good alternative to Riso & Hudson's book, Personality Types.

Questionnaires

Many questionnaires have been developed to help determine your Enneagram type. Partly because the Enneagram type is determined to such a large extent by motivation and less so by behavior, it appears to be difficult to develop a completely reliable instrument. In my experience, this is partly the reason why it is not possible to rely totally on the conclusions drawn by a questionnaire. However, it can be useful and inspiring as a first attempt to determine the type, so long as we are willing to leave the conclusion open to discussion. Don't be surprised if you are confronted with different conclusions after filling out different questionnaires.

Daniels, D.N. and V.A. Price, *Stanford Enneagram Discover Inventory and Guide,* Mind Garden, Inc., 42 pages, ISBN 0966660102.

The focus of this small book of less than 50 pages is on discovering your own type. Daniels and Price, inspired by Helen Palmer's oral tradition, developed a self-assessment tool that does not consist of a large number of questions, like most others, but consists of nine anecdotes of a few paragraphs each. The reader is asked to indicate which anecdote applies most closely to himself. The preferred anecdote indicates the presumed type of the reader. It seems that those who choose the type 1 anecdote have a 66% chance of being a 1 themselves. Eight percent of readers are likely to be in error and are more likely to be a 4. A further 8% are 6s, 7% are 2s and 5%, 9s. The validation for these conclusions is derived from research with around 1,000 candidates who filled in the inventory and subsequently attended an intensive Enneagram workshop. The conclusions of the trainer or the participant himself after the workshop are considered the standard.

Riso, D.R. and R. Hudson, *The Riso-Hudson Enneagram Type Indicator,* Version 2.0, Don Richard Riso, 1997, 17 pages.

This questionnaire contains of 144 questions consisting of two statements. You are asked to indicate which statement is most applicable to yourself. Riso and Hudson have also published the same questionnaire on their website, which also calculates the results. It is possible that the second or third score is not far off the top score. Don't be distracted by the highest score, but consider the three highest scores as possible options for the type that is most likely to be yours. The authors declare that an accuracy of 85-90% is possible if you follow the instructions for filling in the questionnaire properly. No indication is given of what these figures are based on.

Wuchner, S. and D. Wright, *The Enneagram Cards,* Ave Maria Press, 1994, 087793522x.

The intention of this card game is to help you define your type. The user is asked to select cards that apply to him and this then leads to a specific type. The selection process is a sort of two-step process and this is where the weakness lies. You are first of all asked to make a selection from a pile of three kinds of cards. One kind of card relates to the doing types 2, 3 and 4. Another relates to the emotional types 8, 9 and 1. And the third kind relates to the perceiving types 5, 6 and 7. It is my experience that people sometimes arrive at a different category in this first part of the process than the segment where their final number belongs. This is not surprising, because the types within the categories have in fact strong similarities in their orientation towards life, but are nevertheless very different. The second step is the selection of cards within the three types left over. My suggestion in using this game would be to skip the first step, and make a selection from the cards for all of the types. Presumably this increases the chances of hitting the right one. A card game is a creative way of developing a questionnaire. If the game is used as described above, there is certainly much pleasure and insight to be gained from it.

Enneagram Personality Decoder, Dynamo House Pty. Ltd., ISBN 187610001x.

A nice thing to have, for which the publishers apparently not deem it worth naming the author. The Decoder is made of a folded, plastic-coated board with two moveable disks inside, and is no larger than 15x15 cm. About 40 questions are answered with yes or no answers, intended to lead to definition of the right type. The explanation of the answers leads me to the assumption that the Decoder is based on Riso's approach.

ABOUT THE AUTHOR

After graduating in Organizational Psychology from the University of Amsterdam, Oscar David became self-employed. Since 1989, he has provided his services for almost all of the top 20 multinationals in the Netherlands.

Oscar David is widely known in the Netherlands as a leading Management Consultant for executive development, leadership and team building. The first certified Enneagram trainer in the Netherlands, since 1993 he has introduced the system to several thousands of managers and professionals in companies like Shell, Philips, ABN AMRO

Bank, Price Waterhouse Coopers, ING Bank, KPMG, Wolters Kluwer (publishing), Getronics Wang, Hoogovens (steel manufacturing), Ahold (supermarket chain in the US, Europe and Asia), Telfort (British Telecom), and Libertel-Vodafone (telecom) as well as organizations like the Police Force and the Ministry of Finance in The Netherlands.

Oscar David uses the Enneagram as a tool in team-building programs, executive coaching, and management development programs and as part of organizational change activities.

Oscar David Consultancy
Van Eeghenstraat 101
1071 EZ Amsterdam
The Netherlands

Tel. ++ (31) (20) 4004 310
Fax ++ (31) (20) 4004 320
Email: info@oscardavid.nl

www.oscardavid.com
www.enneagramacademy.com

9 780595 195466

17715417R00106

Made in the USA
Lexington, KY
24 September 2012